WORLD INEQUALITY

Origins and Perspectives on The World System

WORLD INEQUALITY

ORIGINS AND PERSPECTIVES ON THE WORLD SYSTEM

edited by Immanuel Wallerstein

BLACK ROSE BOOKS   Montréal

BLACK ROSE BOOKS NO. E 26

First Edition in English 1975

Hardcover — ISBN: 0-919618-66-9
Paperback — ISBN: 0-919618-65-0

Cover Design: Michael Carter

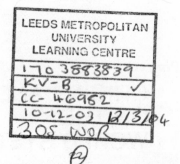

Canadian Cataloguing in Publication Data
Main entry under title:

World inequality

ISBN 0-919618-66-9 bd.
ISBN 0-919618-65-0 pa.

1. Equality—Addresses, essays, lectures.
2. Social conflict—Addresses, essays, lectures.
3. Economic development—Addresses, essays, lectures.
1. Wallerstein, Immanuel, 1930-

HC59.7.W67   301.6   C76-015114-1

Translation from the French by Ferry de Kerckhove and Immanuel Wallerstein

BLACK ROSE BOOKS LTD.
3934 rue St.Urbain,
Montréal 131, Québec

Printed and bound in Québec, Canada

CONTENTS

4/ Cultural Aspects

PREFACE

INEQUALITY is an old theme. Before the modern world, it was usually considered an inevitable reality of human existence. Egalitarian movements tended to take a religious garb, and frequently concluded that the solution was not to be found in the city of man, but in the city of God.

The French Revolution was world-shaking in many ways. One way was that it was the expression of a secular movement which proclaimed equality as a realizable political goal. And in the nineteenth century, there were many movements that struggled to achieve equality: nationalist movements which asserted that every "nation" had an equal right to be free; social movements which asserted that within a nation opportunity (and/or distribution of wealth) should be equal.

But the nineteenth century world was in two ways intellectually constrained. It was Europocentric. And it assumed that the primary framework of social action was the nation-state. The events of the twentieth century have shredded these assumptions. Europe's centrality turned out to be inescapably a momentary phenomenon. And the nation-state has turned out not to be an autonomous unit of social action and to have virtually no possibility of becoming one. The remedy to inequality turned out not to lie within the nation-state but within the world-system as a whole. Thus both national and even *inter*national action have their inherent limitations, if we wish to understand and affect the capitalist *world*-economy.

This then was the framewok of analysis for the colloquium, convened in Montreal from May 15-18, 1974 by the Centre Québécois des Relations Internationales and the Research Commission, National Movements and Imperialism of the International Sociological Association. The hope was to bring into one framework two arenas of discussion which have had a long history. All papers in this book were presented at the colloquium except that of Prof. Mel Watkins. One arena was that of social conflict in the industrialized world: the class struggle, the role of labour and socialist movements, evolutionary versus revolutionary theories of change, the nature of the Russian Revolution. The second arena was that of the revolt of the Third World: anti-imperialism, the roots of "underdevelopment," the struggles for national liberation, the ways in which the Chinese Revolution differed from the Russian.

It was the belief of the organizers that these two debates were really a single one because they reflected different aspects of a single historical phenomenon, the functioning of the capitalist world-economy which is the modern world-system.

This book then is organized in a very straightforward way. The opening essay seeks to make clear the distinction between a "world-system" perspective believed to provide the appropriate basis for analysis and an older way of thinking going back to nineteenth-century ways of analysis which is called the "developmentalist" perspective. The succeeding papers are analyses, more or less within a world-system perspective, of the sources and structure of world inequality in the economic, political and cultural arenas of the world-system, and prospects for the future.

In the course of these analyses, the authors seek to look anew at some familiar themes: economic development, the role of the state, the political struggles of the working class, the nature of unity or pan-movements, the Chinese Cultural Revolution.

The reader will observe that even when operating within a single overall perspective the authors still find much to disagree about. Some of the disagreements seem definitional. Are "socialist states" in or out of the capitalist world-economy? To what extent is there socialist content in national liberation movements? Are the unionized workers in highly industrialized countries a potentially "revolutionary" class? Is the Great Proletatian Cultural Revolution an expression of cultural nationalism or of class struggle?

The source of these disagreements seem to me to be in the implications particular arguments have for the tactics of the struggle. If we wish to work to destroy world inequality, how do we best do it? What are the natural alliances?

This book in no way answers those questions. It seeks to make it possible to come to grips with them intelligently by clearing away some of the intellectual confusion which has blinded us to our real choices, and which has been encouraged by those who wish to perpetuate rather than to destroy world inequality.

The colloquium was held in Québec in Canada. Both Québec and Canada have in recent years exemplified the coming together of the two arenas of analysis: social conflict in the industrialized world, and the revolt of the Third World.

In 1945, or even 1965, it would have seemed incredible to most Québécois or most Canadians to think of either Québec or Canada as part of the Third World, even metaphorically. In 1975, it was a point of view espoused by a number of writers. And yet, both Québec and Canada rank high on measures of industrialization and standard of living. The internal social struggles seem in many ways similar to those that occur in Western Europe or the United States.

Perhaps, as our understanding of the implications of a world-system perspective spreads, what now seems to many anomalous in the situation of Québec and Canada will fit more clearly into place. Perhaps by looking at Brazil and the United States afresh as integral parts of a functioning capitalist world-economy, we will be more able to look afresh at Québec and Canada.

With greater clarity of analysis may come greater force of struggle against the institutions that sustain world inequality — in Québec, in Canada, elsewhere in the world.

Immanuel Wallerstein

THE PRESENT STATE OF THE DEBATE ON WORLD INEQUALITY

Immanuel Wallerstein

IT has never been a secret from anyone that some have more than others. And in the modern world at least, it is no secret that some countries have more than other countries. In short, world inequality is a phenomenon about which most men and most groups are quite conscious.

I do not believe that there has ever been a time when these inequalities were unquestioned. That is to say, people or groups who have more have always felt the need to justify this fact, if for no other reason than to try to convince those who have less that they should accept this fact with relative docility. These ideologies of the advantaged have had varying degrees of success over time. The history of the world is one of a constant series of revolts against inequality — whether that of one people or nation vis-à-vis another or of one class within a geographical area against another.

This statement is probably true of all of recorded history, indeed of all historical events, at least since the Neolithic Revolution. What has changed with the advent of the modern world in the 16th century is neither the existence of inequalities nor of the felt need to justify them by means of ideological constructs. What has changed is that even those who defend the "inevitability" of inequalities in the present feel the need to argue that eventually, over time, these inequalities will disappear, or at the very least diminish considerably in scope. Another way of saying this is that of the three dominant ideological currents of the modern world — conservatism, liberalism, and Marxism — two at least (liberalism and Marxism) are committed in theory and the abstract to egalitarianism as a principle. The third, conservatism, is not, but conservatism is an ideology that has been very much on the defensive ever since the French revolution. The proof of this is that most conservatives decline to fly the banner openly but hide their conservative ideas under the mantle of liberalism or occasionally even Marxism.

Surely it is true that in the universities of the world in the 20th century, and in other expressions of intellectuals, the contending ideologies have been one variant or another of liberalism and Marxism. (Remember at this point we are talking of ideologies and not of political movements. Both "Liberal" parties and Social-Democratic parties in the 20th century have drawn on liberal ideologies.)

One of the most powerful thrusts of the 18th-century Enlightenment, picked up by most 19th and 20th century thought-systems, was the assumption of progress, reformulated later as evolution. In the context of the question of equality, evolution was interpreted as the process of moving from an imperfect, unequal allocation of privileges and resources to some version of equality. There was considerable argument about how to define equality. (Reflect on the different meanings of "equality of opportunity" and "to each according to his needs.") There was considerable disagreement about who or what were the obstacles to this desired state of equality. And there was fundamental discord about how to transform the world from its present imperfection to the desired future, primarily between the advocates of gradualism based on education to advocates of revolution based on the use at some point in time of violence.

I review this well-know history of modern ideas simply to underline where I think our current debates are simply the latest variant of now classic debates and where I think some new issues have been raised which make these older formulations outdated.

If one takes the period 1945-1960, both politically and intellectually, we have in many ways the apogee of the liberal-Marxist debate. The world was politically polarized in the so-called cold war. There were two camps. One called itself the "free world" and argued that it and it alone upheld the first part of the French Revolution's trilogy, that of "liberty." It argued that its economic system offered the hope over time of approximating "equality" through a path which it came to call "economic development" or sometimes just "development." It argued too that it was gradually achieving "fraternity" by means of education and political reform (such as the 1954 Supreme Court decision in the United States, ending the legality of segregation.)

The other camp called itself the "socialist world" and argued that it and it alone represented the three objectives of the French Revolution and hence the interests of the people of the world. It argued that when movements inspired by these ideas would come to power in all non-"socialist" countries, (and however they came to power,) each would enact legislation along the same lines and by this process the whole world would become "socialist" and the objective would be achieved.

These somewhat simplistic ideological statements were of course developed in much more elaborate form by the intellectuals. It has become almost traditional (but I think nonetheless just) to cite W.W. Rostow's *The Stages of Economic Growth* as a succinct, sophisticated, and relatively pure expression of the dominant liberal ideology which informed the thinking of the political leadership of the United States and its Western allies. Rostow showed no modesty in his subtitle: which was "a non-Communist Manifesto."

His basic thesis is no doubt familiar to most persons interested in these problems. Rostow saw the process of change as a series of stages through which each national unit had to go. They were the stages through which Rostow felt Great Britain had gone, and Great Britain was the crucial example since it was defined as being the first state to embark on the evolutionary path of the modern industrial world. The inference, quite overtly drawn, was that this path was a model, to be copied by other states. One could then analyze what it took to move from one stage to another, why some nations took longer than others, and could prescribe (like a physician) what a nation must do to hurry along its process of "growth." I will not review what ideological function such a formulation served. This has been done repeatedly and well. Nonetheless, this viewpoint, somewhat retouched, still informs the developmentalist ideas of the major Western governments as well as that of international agencies. I consider Lester Pearson's "Partners in Progress" report in the direct line of this analytic framework.

In the socialist world in this period there was no book quite the match of Rostow's. What there was instead was an encrusted version of evolutionary Marxism which also saw rigid stages through which every state or geographical entity had to go. The differences were that the stages covered longer historical time and the model country was the USSR. These are the stages known as slavery-feudalism-capitalism-socialism. The absurdities of the rigid formulation which dates from the 1930's and the inappropriateness of applying this on a *national* level have been well argued recently by an Indian Marxist intellectual, Irfan Habib, who argues not only the meaningfulness of the concept of the "Asiatic mode of production" but also the illogic of insisting that the various historical modes of extracting a surplus must each, necessarily, occur in all countries and follow in a specific order. Habib argues:

> The materialist conception of history need not necessarily prescribe a set universal periodisation, since what it essentially does is to formulate an analytic method for the development of class societies, and any periodisation, theoretically, serves as no more than the illustration of the application of such a method... The crucial thing is the definition of principal contradiction (i.e., class-contradictions) in a society, the marking out of factors responsible for intensifying them, and the deliniation of the shaping of the social order, when a particular contradiction is resolved. It is possible that release from the set P-S-F-C- pattern [primitive communism-slavery-feudalism-capitalism] may lead Marxists to apply themselves better to this task, since they would no longer be obliged to look for the same 'fundamental laws of the epoch' (a favourite Soviet term), or 'prime mover', as premised for the supposedly corresponding European epoch.[1]

I give this excerpt from Habib because I very much agree with his fundamental point that this version of Marxist thought, so prevalent between 1945 and 1965, is a sort of "mechanical copying" of liberal views. Basically, the analysis is the same as that represented by Rostow except that the names of the stages are changed and the model country has shifted from Great Britain to the USSR. I will call this approach the developmentalist perspective, as espoused either by liberals or Marxists.

There is another perspective that has slowly pushed its way into public view during the 1960's. It has no commonly-accepted name, in part because the early formulations of this point of view have often been confused, partial, or unclear. It was first widely-noticed in the thinking of the Latin American structuralists (such as Prebisch and Furtado) and those allied to them elsewhere (such as

Dudley Seers). It later took the form of arguments such as the "development of underdevelopment" (A.G. Frank, in the heritage of Baran's *The Political Economy of Growth*), the "structure of dependence" (Theontonio Dos Santos), "unequal exchange" (Arghiri Emmanuel), "accumulation of world capital" (Samir Amin), "subimperialism" (Ruy Mauro Marini). It also surfaced in the Chinese Cultural Revolution as Mao's concept of the continuity of the class struggle under socialist regimes in single countries.[2]

What all these concepts have in common is a critique of the developmentalist perspective. Usually they make it from a Marxist tradition but it should be noted that some of the critics, such as Furtado, come from a liberal heritage. It is no accident that this point of view has been expressed largely by persons from Asia, Africa and Latin America or by those others particularly interested in these regions (such as Umberto Melotti of *Terzo Mondo*).[3]

I would like to designate this point of view the "world-system perspective." I mean by that term that it is based on the assumption, explicitly or implicitly, that the modern world comprises a single capitalist world-economy, which has emerged historically since the sixteenth century and which still exists today. It follows from such a premise that national states are *not* societies that have separate, parallel histories, but parts of a whole reflecting that whole. To the extent that stages exist, they exist for the system as a whole. To be sure, since different parts of the world play and have played differing roles in the capitalist world-economy, they have dramatically different internal socio-economic profiles and hence distinctive politics But to understand the internal class contradictions and political struggles of a particular state, we must first situate it in the world-economy. We can then understand the ways in which various political and cultural thrusts may be efforts to alter or preserve a position within this world-economy which is to the advantage or disadvantage of particular groups located within a particular state.[4]

What thus distinguishes the developmentalist and the world-system perspective is not liberalism versus Marxism nor evolutionism vs. something else (since both are essentially evolutionary). Rather I would locate the distinction in two places. One is in mode of thought. To put it in Hegelian terms, the developmentalist perspective is mechanical, whereas the world-system perspective is dialectical. I mean by the latter term that at every point in the analysis, one asks not what is the formal structure but what is the consequence for both the whole and the parts of maintaining or changing a certain structure at that particular point in time, given the totality of particular positions of that moment in time. Intelligent analysis demands knowledge of the complex texture of social reality (historical concreteness) within a long-range perspective that observes trends and forces of the world-system, which can explain what underlies and informs the diverse historically concrete phenomena. If synchronic comparisons and abstracted generalizations are utilized, it is only as heuristic devices in search of a truth that is ever contemporary and hence ever-changing.

This distinction of scientific methodology is matched by a distinction of praxis, of the politics of the real world. For what comes through as the second great difference between the two perspectives (the developmentalist and the world-system) is the prognosis for action. This is the reason why the latter perspective has emerged primarily from the intellectuals of the Third World. The developmentalist perspective not only insists that the model is to be found in the old developed countries (whether Great Britain — U.S.A. or U.S.S.R.) but also that the fundamental international political issues revolve around the relations among the hegemonic powers of the world. From a world-system perspective, there are no "models" (a mechanical notion) and the relations of the hegemonic powers are only one of many issues that confront the world-system.

The emergence of the world-system perspective is a consequence of the dramatic challenge to European political domination of the world which has called into question all Europo-centric constructions of social reality. But intellectual evolution itself is seldom dramatic. The restructuring of the allocation of power in the world has made itself felt in the realm of ideas, particularly in the hegemonic areas of the world, via a growing malaise that intellectuals in Europe (including of course North America) have increasingly felt about the validity of their answers to a series of "smaller" questions — smaller, that is, than the nature of the world-system as such.

Let us review successively six knotty questions to which answers from a developmentalist perspective have increasingly seemed inadequate.

Why have certain world-historical events of the last two centuries taken place where and when they have? The most striking "surprise", at the moment it occurred and ever since, is the Russian Revolution. As we all know, neither Marx nor Lenin nor anyone else though that a "socialist revolution" would occur in Russia earlier than anywhere else. Marx had more or less predicted Great Britain as the likely candidate, and after Marx's death, the consensus of expectation in the international socialist movement was that it would occur in Germany. We know that even after 1917 almost all the leading figures of the CPSU expected that the "revolution" would have to occur quickly in Germany if the Soviet regime was to survive. There was however no socialist revolution in Germany and nonetheless the Soviet regime did survive.

We do not want for explanations of this phenomenon, but we do lack convincing answers. Of course, there exists an explanation that turns Marx on his head and argues that socialist revolutions occur not in the so-called "advanced capitalist" countries but precisely in "backward" countries. But this is in such blatant contradiction with other parts of the developmentalist perspective that its proponents are seldom willing to state it baldly, even less defend it openly.

Nor is the Russian Revolution the only anomaly. There is a long-standing debate about the "exceptionalism" of the United States. How can we explain that the U.S.A. replaced Great Britain as the hegemonic industrial power of the world, and in the process managed to avoid giving birth to a serious internal socialist movement? And if the U.S.A. could avoid socialism, why could not Brazil or Russia or Canada? Seen from the perspective of 1800, it would have been a bold social scientist who would have predicted the particular success of the U.S.A.

Again there have been many explanations. There is the "frontier" theory. There is the theory that underlines the absence of a previously entrenched "feudal" class. There is the theory of the U.S. as Britain's "junior partner" who overtook the senior. But all of these theories are precisely "exceptionalist" theories, contradicting the developmentalist paradigm. And furthermore, some of these variables apply to other countries where they did not seem to have the same consequences.

We could go on. I will mention two more briefly. For a long time, Great Britain's primacy (the "first" industrial power) has been unquestioned. But was Britain the "first" and if so why was she? This is a question that only recently has been seriously adumbrated. In April 1974 at another international colloquium held here in Montreal on the theme of "Failed Transitions to Industrialism: The Case of 17th Century Netherlands and Renaissance Italy", one view put forward quite strongly was that neither Italy nor the Netherlands was the locus of the Industrial Revolution precisely because they were too far *advanced* economically. What a striking blow to a developmentalist paradigm.

And lastly one should mention the anomaly of Canada: a country which economically falls into a category below that of the world's leading industrial producers in structural terms, yet nonetheless is near the very top of the list in per capita income. This cannot be plausibly explained from a developmentalist perspective.

If the world has been "developing" or "progressing" over the past few centuries, how do we explain the fact that in many areas things seem to have gotten worse, not better? Worse in many ways, ranging from standard of living, to the physical environment, to the quality of life. And more to the point, worse in some places but better in others. I refer not merely to such contemporary phenomena as the so-called "growing gap" between the industrialized countries and the Third World, but also to such earlier phenomena as the deindustrialization of many areas of the world (starting with the widely-known example of the Indian textile industry in the late 18th and early 19th century.)

You may say that this contradicts the liberal version of the developmentalist perspective but not its Marxist version, since "polarization" was seen as part of the process of change. True enough, except that "polarization" was presumably within countries and not between them. Furthermore, it is not clear that it is "polarization" that has occurred. While the rich have gotten richer and the poor have gotten poorer, there is surely a fairly large group of countries now somewhere in between on many economic criteria, to cite such politically diverse examples as Mexico, Italy, Czechoslovakia, Iran, and South Africa.

Furthermore, we witness in the 1970's a dramatic shift in the distribution of the profit and the international terms of trade of oil (and possibly other raw materials.) You may say it is because of the increased political sophistication and strength of the Arab world. No doubt this has occurred, but is this an explanation? I remind this group that the last moment of time in which there was a dramatic amelioration of world terms of trade of primary products was in the period 1897-1913, a moment which represented in political terms the apogee of European colonial control of the world.

Once again it is not that there are not a large number of explanations for the rise in oil prices. It is rather than I find these explanations, for what they're worth, in contradiction with a developmentalist perspective.

Why are there "regressions?" In 1964, S.N. Eisenstadt published an article entitled "Breakdowns of Modernization," in which he discussed the fact that there seemed to be cases of "reversal" of regimes to "a lower, less flexible level of political and social differentiation...."[5]

In seeking explain the origins of such "reversals," Eisenstadt restricted himself to hesitant hypotheses:

> The problem of why in Turkey, Japan, Mexico, and Russia there emerge in the initial stages of modernization elites with orientations to change and ability to implement relatively effective policies, while they did not develop in these initial phases in Indonesia, Pakistan, or Burma, or why elites with similar differences tended to develop also in later stages of modernization, is an extremely difficult one and constitutes one of the most baffling problems in comparative sociological analysis. There are but four available indications to deal with this problem. Very tentatively, it may perhaps be suggested that to some extent it has to do with the placement of these elites in the preceding social structure, with the extent of their internal cohesiveness, and of the internal transformation of their own value orientation.[6]

As is clear, Eisenstadt's tentative explanation is to be found in anterior factors operating internally in the state. This calls into question the concept of stages through which all not only must pass but all *can* pass, but it leaves intact the state framework as the focus of analysis and explanation. This of course leads us logically to ask how these anterior factors developed. Are they pure historical accident?

Similarly after the political rebellion of Tito's Yugoslavia against the U.S.S.R., the latter began to accuse Yugoslavia of "revisionism" and of returning to capitalism. Later, China took up the same theme against the U.S.S.R.

But how can we explain how this happens? There are really two varieties of explanation from a developmentalist perspective. One is to say that "regression" seems to have occurred, but that in fact "progress" had never taken place. The leaders of a movement, whether a nationalist movement or a socialist movement, only pretented to favor change. In fact they were really always "neo-colonialist" stooges or "revisionists" at heart. Such an explanation has partial truth, but it seems to me to place too much on "false consciousness" and to fail to analyze movements in their immediate and continuing historical contexts.

The second explanation of "regression" is a change of heart — "betrayal." Yes, but once again, how come sometimes, but not always? Are we to explain large-scale social phenomena on the basis of the accident of the biographic histories of the particular leaders involved? I cannot accept this, for leaders remain leaders in the long run only if their personal choices reflect wider social pressures.

If the fundamental paradigm of modern history is a series of parallel national processes, how do we explain the persistence of nationalism, indeed quite often its primacy, as a political force in the modern world? Developmentalists who are liberals deplore nationalism or explain it away as a transitional "integrating" phenomenon. Marxists who are developmentalists are even more embarassed. If the class struggle is primary — that is, implicitly the intra-national class struggle — how do we explain the fact that the slogan of the Cuban revolution is "Patria o muerte — venceremos?" And how could we explain this even more astonishing quotation from Kim Il Sung, the leader of the Democratic People's Republic of Korea:

> The homeland is a veritable mother for everyone. We cannot live nor be happy outside of our homeland. Only the flourishing and prosperity of our homeland will permit us to go down the path to happiness. The best sons and daughters of our people, all without exception, were first of all ardent patriots. It was to recover their homeland that Korean Communists struggled, before the Liberation, against Japanese imperialism despite every difficulty and obstacle. [7]

And if internal processes are so fundamental, why has not the reality of international workers' solidarity been greater? Remember the First World War.

As before, there are many explanations for the persistence of nationalism. I merely observe that all these explanations have to *explain away* the primacy of internal national processes. Or to put it another way, for developmentalists nationalism is sometimes good, sometimes bad. But when it is the one or the other, it is ultimately explained by developmentalists in an ad hoc manner, adverting to its meaning for the world-system.

An even more difficult problem for the developmentalists has been the recrudescence of nationalist movements in areas smaller than that of existing states. And it is not Biafra of Bangladesh that is an intellectual problem, because the usual manner of accounting for secessionist movements in Third World countries has been the failure to attain the stage of "national integration."

No, the surprise has been in the industrialized world: Blacks in the U.S.A., Québec in Canada, Occitania in France, the Celts in Great Britain, and lurking in the background the nationalities question in the U.S.S.R. It is not that any of these "nationalisms" is new. They are all long-standing themes of political and cultural conflict in all these countries. The surprise has been that, as of say 1945 or even 1960, most persons in these countries, using a developmentalist paradigm, regarded these movements or claims as remnants of a dying past, destined to diminish still further in vitality. And lo, a phœnix reborn.

The explanations are there. Some cry, anachronism — but if so, then the question remains, how come such a flourishing anachronism? Some say, loud shouting but little substance, a last bubble of national integration. Perhaps, but the intellectual and organizational development of these ethno-national movements seem to have moved rapidly and ever more firmly in a direction quite opposite to national integration. In any case, what in the developmentalist paradigm explains this phenomenon?

One last question, which is perhaps only a reformulation of the previous five. How is it that the "ideal types" of the different versions of the developmentalist perspective all seem so far from empirical reality? Who has not had the experience of not being quite certain which party represents the "industrial proletariat" or the "modernizing elite" in Nigeria, or in France of the Second Empire for that matter? Let us be honest. Each of us, to the extent that he has ever used a developmentalist paradigm, has stretched empirical reality to a very Procrustean bed indeed.

Can the world-system perspective answer these questions better? We cannot yet be sure. This point of view has not yet been fully thought through. But let me indicate some possible lines of argument.

If the world-system is the focus of analysis, and if in particular we are talking of the capitalist world-economy, then divergent historical patterns are precisely to be expected. They are not an anomaly but the essence of the system. If the world-economy is the basic economic entity comprising a single division of labor, then it is natural that different areas perform different economic tasks. Anyway it is natural under capitalism, and we may talk of the core, the periphery and the semi-periphery of the world-economy. Since however political boundaries (states) are smaller than the economic whole, they will each reflect different groupings of economic tasks and strengths in the world-market. Over time, some of these differences may be accentuated rather than diminished — the basic inequalities which are our theme of discussion.

It is also clear that over time the loci of economic activities keep changing. This is due to many factors — ecological exhaustion, the impact of new technology, climate changes, and the socioeconomic consequences of these "natural" phenomena. Hence some areas "progress" and others "regress." But the fact that particular states change their position in the world-economy, from semi-periphery to core say, or vice versa, does not in itself change the nature of the system. These shifts will be registered for individual states as "development" or "regression." The key factor to note is that within a capitalist world-economy, all states cannot "develop" simultaneously *by definition*, since the system functions by virtue of having unequal core and peripheral regions.[8]

Within a world-economy, the state structures function as ways for particular groups to affect and distort the functioning of the market. The stronger the state-machinery, the more its ability to distort the world-market in favor of the interests it represents. Core states have stronger state-machineries than peripheral states.

This role of the state machineries in a capitalist world-economy explains the persistence of nationalism, since the primary social conflicts are quite often between groups located in different states rather than between groups located within the same state-boundaries. Furthermore, this explains the ambiguity of class as a concept, since class refers to the economy which is world-wide, but class consciousness is a political, hence primarily national, phenomenon. Within this context, one can see the recrudescence of ethno-nationalisms in industrialized states as an expression of class consciousness of lower caste-class groups in societies where the class terminology has been preempted by nation-wide middle strata organized around the dominant ethnic group.

If then the world-system is the focus of analysis rather than the individual states, it is the natural history of this system at which we must look. Like all systems, the capitalist world-economy has both cyclical and secular trends, and it is important to distinguish them.

On the one hand, the capitalist world-economy seems to go through long cycles of "expansion" and "contraction." I cannot at this point go into the long discussion this would require. I will limit myself to the very brief suggestion that "expansion" occurs when the totality of world production is less than world effective demand, as permitted by the existing social distribution of world purchasing power, and that "contraction" occurs when total world production exceeds world effective demand. These are cycles of 75-100 years in length in my view and the downward cycle is only resolved by a political reallocation of world income that effectively expands world demand. I believe we have just ended an expansionary cycle and we are in the beginning of a contractual one.

These cycles occur within a secular trend that has involved the physical expansion and politico-structural consolidation of the capitalist world-economy as such, but has also given birth to forces and movements which are eating away at these same structural supports of the existing world-system. In particular, these forces which we call revolutionary forces are calling into question the phenomenon of inequality so intrinsic to the existing world-system.

The trend towards structural consolidation of the system over the past four centuries has included three basic developments:

The first has been the capitalization of world agriculture, meaning the ever more efficient use of the world's land and sea resources in large productive units with larger and larger components of fixed capital. Over time, this has encompassed more and more of the earth's surface, and at the present we are probably about to witness the last major physical expansion, the elimination of all remaining plots restricted to small-scale, so-called "subsistence" production. The counterpart of this process has been the steady concentration of the world's population as salaried workers in small, dense pockets —

that is, proletarianization and urbanization. The initial impact of this entire process has been to render large populations more exploitable and controllable.

The second major structural change has been the development of technology that maximizes the ability to transform the resources of the earth into useable commodities at "reasonable" cost levels. This is what we call industrialization, and the story is far from over. The next century should see the spread of industrial activity from the temperate core areas in which it has hitherto been largely concentrated to the tropical and semi-tropical peripheral areas. Industrialization too has hitherto tended to consolidate the system in providing a large part of the profit that makes the system worth the while of those who are on top of it, with a large enough surplus to sustain and appease the world's middle strata. Mere extension of industrial activity will not change a peripheral area into a core area, for the core areas will concentrate on ever newer, specialized activities.

The third major development, at once technological and social, has been the strengthening of all organizational structures — the states, the economic corporate structures, and even the cultural institutions — vis-à-vis both individuals and groups. This is the process of bureaucratization, and while it has been uneven (the core states are still stronger than the peripheral states, for example), all structures are stronger today than previously. Prime ministers of contemporary states have the power today that Louis XIV sought in vain to achieve. This too has been stabilizing because the ability of these bureaucracies physically to repress opposition is far greater than in the past.

But there is the other side of each of these coins. The displacement of the world's population into urban areas has made it easier ultimately to organize forces against the power structures. This is all the more so since the ever-expanding market-dependent, propertyless groups are simultaneously more educated, more in communication with each other, and hence *potentially* more politically conscious.

The steady industrialization of the world has eaten away at the political and hence economic justifications for differentials in rewards. The technological advances, while still unevenly distributed, have created a new military equality of destructive potential. It is true that one nation may have 1000 times the fire power of another, but if the weaker one has sufficient to incur grievous damage, of how much good is it for the stronger to have 1000 times as much strength? Consider not merely the power of a weaker state with a few nuclear rockets but the military power of urban guerillas. It is the kind of problem Louis XIV precisely did *not* need to worry about.

Finally, the growth of bureaucracies in the long run has created the weakness of topheaviness. The ability of the presumed decision-makers to control not the populace but the bureaucracies has effectively diminished, which again creates a weakness in the ability to enforce politico-economic will.

Where then in this picture do the forces of change, the movements of liberation, come in? They come in precisely as not totally coherent pressures of groups which arise out of the structural contradictions of the capitalist world-economy. These groups seem to take organizational form as movements, as parties, and sometimes as regimes. But when the movements become regimes, they are caught in the dilemma of becoming part of the machinery of the capitalist world-economy they are presuming to change. Hence the so-called "betrayals." It is important neither to adulate blindly these regimes, for inevitably they "betray" in part their stated goals, nor to be cynical and despairing, for the movements which give birth to such regimes represent real forces, and the creation of such regimes is part of a long-run process of social transformation.

What we need to put in the forefront of our consciousness is that both the party of order and the party of movement are currently strong. We have not yet reached the peak of the political consolidation of the capitalist world-economy. We are already in the phase of its political decline. If your outlook is developmentalist and mechanical, this pair of statements is an absurdity. From a world-system perspective, and using a dialectical mode of analysis, it is quite precise and intelligible.

This struggle takes place on all fronts — political, economic, and cultural — and in all arenas of the world, in the core states, in the periphery (largely in the Third World), and in the semi-periphery (many but not all of which states have collective ownership of basic property and are hence often called "socialist" states).

Take a struggle like that of Vietnam, or Algeria, or Angola. They were wars of national liberation. They united peoples in these areas. Ultimately, the forces of national liberation won or are winning political change. How may we evaluate its effect? On the one hand, these colonial wars fundamentally weakened the internal supports of the regimes of the U.S.A., France and Portugal. They sapped the dominant forces of world capitalism. These wars made many changes possible in the countries of struggle, the metropolises, and in third countries. And yet, and yet — one can ask if the net result has not been in part further to integrate these countries, even their regimes, into the capitalist world-economy. It did both of course. We gain nothing by hiding this from ourselves. On the other hand, we gain nothing by showing olympian neutrality in the form of equal disdain for unequal combatants.

The process of analysis and the process of social transformation are not separate. They are obverse sides of one coin. Our praxis informs, indeed makes possible, our analytic frameworks. But the work of analysis is itself a central part of the praxis of change. The perspectives for the future of inequality in the world-system are fairly clear in the long run. In the long-run the inequalities will disappear as the result of a fundamental transformation of the world-system. But we all live in the short run, not in the long run. And in the short run, within the constraints of our respective social locations and our social heritages, we labor in the vineyards as we wish, towards what ends we choose. We are here today because we want to be. We will make of this colloquium what we want to make of it, and we will draw whatever political conclusions we wish to draw.

NOTES

(1) Irfan Habib, "Problems of Marxist Historical Analysis in India," *Enquiry*, Monsoon, 1969, reprinted in S.A. Shah, ed., *Towards National Liberation: Essays on the Political Economy of India* (Montreal: n.p., 1973), 8-9.
(2) See my "Class Struggle in China?", *Monthly Review*, XXV, 4, Sept. 1973, 55-58.
(3) See U. Melotti, "Marx e il Terzo Mondo," *Terzo Mondo*, No. 13-14, sett.-dict. 1971. Melitto subtitles the work: "towards a multilinear schema of the Marxist conception of historical development."
(4) I have developed this argument at length elsewhere. See *The Modern World-System: Capitalist Agriculture and the Origins of the European World-Economy* (New York and London: Academic Press, 1974) and "The Rise and Future Demise of the World Capitalist System: Concepts for Comparative Analysis," *Comparative Studies in Society and History*, XVI, 4, Oct., 1974, 387-415.
(5) S.N. Eisenstadt, "Breakdowns of Modernization," *Economic Development and Cultural Change*, XII, 4, July 1964, 367.

(6) *Ibid.*, pp. 365-366.
(7) *Activité Révolutionnaire du Camarade Kim Il Sung* (Pyongyang: Ed. en langues étrangères, 1970). Livre illustré, 52nd page (edition unpaginated). Translation mine – I.W.
(8) As to how particular states can change their position, I have tried to furnish an explanation in "Dependence in an Interdependent World: The Limited Possibilities of Transformation Within the Capitalist World-Economy," *African Studies Review*, XVII, 1, April 1974, 1-26.

WORLD INEQUALITY:
economic aspects

HEGEMONIC POWERS IN THE CONTEMPORARY WORLD

Richard D. Wolff

WHILE today any discussion of hegemonic capitalism must begin with the United States, the desire to place the tendency towards hegemony in perspective suggests a different starting point. Two epochs in the history of capitalist Britain's hegemony in the nineteenth and twentieth centuries will be analyzed. Essential features of these two epochs, taken together as a "model" of development, will permit comparisons with post-1945 history which can provide a helpful perspective on the current condition of the hegemonic capitalist powers.

From the collapse of Napoleon to the 1870's, Britain and British capitalism enjoyed hegemonic power in much of the world. In this epoch, Britain fostered free trade, confident in the competitive victory of British manufactures worldwide. Such confidence extended, after the repeal of the Corn Laws in 1846, even to the point of permitting the steady contraction of nearly all aspects of domestic agriculture. Exports were the leading edge of capitalist development. The dependence on distant markets that this implied was matched by a rapidly growing dependence on imports of food and industrial raw materials. Britain willingly enmeshed herself in an increasingly complicated world-wide division of labour.

Britain's competitive superiority, together with the closely allied financial and military (essentially naval) superiority, provided the three bases of her hegemonic position in this epoch. Each reinforced the other. The resulting strength could and did permit a massive export of capital and capital goods. While such capital flows were necessarily linked to both exports and imports, the fact that they might strengten potential competitors seemed to have little effect. Trade was the engine of capitalist growing and the pound sterling was the lubricant of the engine.

In this context, colonies could come to be seen as "millstones around our necks" as Disraeli complained. David Richardo's little "proof" that by reason of comparative advantage free trade almost necessarily means gains for all participants could become liberal dogma. The point, however, was that anti-colonial-ism and free-tradism were simply expressions of the hegemonic position of the economically most advanced capitalism of the time. Britain not only saw no economic need for her to retain her own colonial territories, she also strenuously opposed colonies for any other state. The economic realities of Britain's interdependent position would necessitate reconsideration of her anti-colonialist policies if and when other states undertook colonization.

In the 1870's British hegemony began to face accelerating competition and challenge. Led by Germany and the United States, but including other states as well, this challenge ushered in the second epoch of British hegemonic power: its period of relative decline.[1] At home and abroad British manufactures faced increasingly successful competition, and consequently the competition spread to include struggle over safe sources of cheap imports of industrial inputs. The complex international division of labor fostered when British capitalism was hegemonic had implied lines of dependence whose security was questioned by the emerging economic, political and military power of Germany, the United States, etc.

From the 1870's to World War I, the challenges to British hegemony stimulated intense debate in England over the costs and benefits of free trade vs. protectionism of various possible types. The agitation for protection culminated in the political career of Joseph Chamberlain at the end of the century. And, as is usual with such debates, not the arguments but the underlying reality determined the outcome.

It has been clearly demonstrated that from the 1870's to World War I, exports accounted for a rapidly growing share of British manufactures, especially in the core industries of textiles, iron and steel products and machinery. [2] It has also been shown that the British Empire accounted for most of this export growth, off-setting the small and relatively stagnant position of British exports in Western Europe and the United States. Further, the statistics indicate that within the Empire the most dynamic, rapidly growing sector absorbing British exports was the "new" Empire, territories acquired in the colonialist scrambles after 1870.

Protectionism in Europe and the United States and the worldwide competition from industries protected there produced a redirection of British exports, the leading edge of British capitalism. Correspondingly, Britain increased the relative importance of Empire territories as sources of food and raw materials. The flows of British capital exports readjusted themselves in line with the shifting commodity flows and the correspondingly shifting political focus of the British governments. [3]

Its economic hegemony undermined, British industry reoriented its trade and capital flow patterns toward the safety of Empire. Yet, the comprehensive imperialism demanded by Chamberlain was decisively rejected. Instead, Britain adopted a half-way position: the size of empire expanded, the economic connections with the empire intensified, but full-scale protectionism was rejected. Britain kept to her free-trade tradition on matters of tariffs, quotas, etc. The City of London financial community (with its trade-connected interests) prevailed over the particular interest of Manchester, the traditional manufacturing center: *some* colonialism would protect the exporters of goods, while *some* free trade would protect the exporters of services, the "invisibles" that made London the financial center of the capitalist world.

To summarize: the challenge to British hegemony redirected the evolving international division of labor into a pattern characterised chiefly by the interplay of competing capitalists striving for hegemony. [4] The intense revival of colonialist policies after 1870 represents a major means then available to implement that striving.

The post-1870 colonialist phase of imperialism involved massive flows of capital into what are now referred to as underdeveloped areas. In almost every case, we can trace the motives for any particular flow to the immediate competitive strategy of a firm, an industry or a government. [5] To safeguard such flows and thus to enhance the competitiveness of Britons, Britain had no choice but to exercise direct authority over more and more territories. Competing capitalist states moved in the same direction. Each feared and anticipated the moves of the other.

Colonialism everywhere provoked economic changes, usually of historic magnitude. It destroyed pre-capitalist economic formations and reorganized societies according to the needs of capitalist states competing for hegemony. This peculiar form of integration into the world economy implied a correspondingly peculiar form of economic development. This pattern has led directly to the world inequality which is the focus of this book's concern.

Inequality, colonialism and the tendency toward hegemony are joint products of capitalism.[6] A particularly intense period of the development of these joint products followed from the accelerated concentration and centralization of capital in Europe and America after 1870.[7] The two epochs of Britain's hegemony, considered together, make a further point that is of special significance in approaching the relation of hegemonic powers and world inequality today.

The imperialism of Britain's hegemonic, free-trade epoch differed fundamentally from the colonialism of the succeeding epoch when her hegemonic position came under increasing challenge. The evolving international division of labor differed; the flows of goods and services and capital differed; the overall economic development of both capitalist metropolises and the underdeveloped periphery differed. I cannot speculate on what might have been in the absence of challenges to British hegemony after 1870. However, what is clear is that post-1870 capitalist colonialism integrated colonies and semi-colonies[8] into a competitive struggle among powers striving for hegemony. That struggle required a specific economic function to be performed by each constituent territory in competing imperial formations. These functions could and did shift, often suddenly, as competing imperial positions shifted. The struggle for hegemony had much to do with World War I and the violent international economic fluctuations of the 1920's and 1930's — all of which administered sudden, traumatic shocks to colonial and semi-colonial territories hardly yet adjusted to the initial consequences of their forced entry into world capitalism. Out of all of this emerged the fact of growing inequality in the world economic system.

Now, with the model of British development in mind, let us turn to an analysis of current hegemonic tendencies.

Leaping over intermediate steps in the analysis; we can divide the post-World War II capitalist world into two epochs comparable to the two epochs of British history examined earlier. The first, extending from the mid-1940's to the late 1960's, encompasses a hegemonic position for the United States. The second, now getting underway, involves challenges to the U.S. position which derive directly or indirectly from Western Europe and from Japan.

Before commencing the analysis, three new phenomena of the international economic scene require specification. Each is the product of tendencies at work earlier which were in fact accelerated by the 1870-1914 epoch of competing capitalisms. First there is the Socialist group of nations: the Soviet Union, Eastern Europe, China, North Korea, North Vietnam and Cuba. In size, in economic significance, and in its political and military power, this group — however disunified — is an important factor on the international economic scene. Second, the revolt and more or less independent movement of African, Asian and Latin American peoples toward the self-determination of their economic and social growth influences the international economy. Third, we observe the multi-national corporate conglomerate, representing the mid-twentieth century result of monopolistic tendencies which first gained momentum within capitalist industry one hundred years earlier. I will return to these three new phenomena as I develop the analysis of post-1945 hegemonic capitalism.

In 1945, the United States had no capitalist rival for hegemony. It only faced two possible obstacles to a smoothly functioning, profitable, worldwide economic hegemony: the socialist block and the colonial revolution. The United States moved quickly, well before World War II ended,[9] to institutionalize its hegemony in the post-1945 capitalist power vacuum. Shortly thereafter, in the later 1940's, the United States acted to contain and, where possible, remove the two obstacles.

The institution of hegemony was accomplished by many interrelated activities of both government and private U.S. firm's military power spread itself through thousands of bases across the globe and especially around the socialist bloc. New York replaced London as the creation of the International Monetary Fund shifted the financial center of world capitalism in line with the new industrial and military center. The United Nations, NATO, CENTO, SEATO and other open and secret formations brought order to the political hegemony implied and required by the U.S. industrial, military and financial superiority. Parallel with these governmental rearrangements, U.S. firms moved quickly and aggressively with direct investments in, as well as exports to, both Europe and the rest of the world.[10] While it is true that "United States policy after the war was to encourage foreign investment,"[11] capital had its own reasons for moving abroad. Rates of return on U.S. direct investment in Europe in the early 1950's ranged from 10.1 per cent in France to 11.9 percent in Germany to 17.2 per cent in the United Kingdom.[12]

Besides military measures and covert operations undertaken against the socialist bloc and revolts in the periphery (in the early 1950's: Korea, Iran, Guatemala, etc.), U.S. hegemonic strategy emphasized the rapid reconstruction and rearmament of Western Europe. The Marshall Plan was meant to stimulate U.S. exports but also to rebuild Western Europe as a subordinate ally against both socialism and revolution in the periphery. From 1946 to 1954, U.S. grants and credits to Western Europe amounted to $25 billion — more than half the net Land-Lease (military equipment, foodstuffs, and industrial material) extended to U.S. allies in World War II.[13] Such was the importance attached to establishing and safeguarding post-war U.S. hegemony.

U.S. hegemony described the context and structure of international economic intercourse from 1945 to the late 1960's. Increasingly the key feature of that intercourse was the multinational corporation, usually but not always based in the United States. Under the hegemonic umbrella, the multinationals went everywhere on the hunt for profits, expanding vertically and horizontally in advanced capitalist countries and in underdeveloped areas. Exports, imports, foreign subsidiaries, minority positions, joint ventures — all were and continue to be aspects of the worldwide spread of multinational enterprise, a form of industrial organization whose competitive superiority was clearly demonstrated in these years.

U.S. hegemony, like Britain's a century earlier, coincided with a revival of anti-colonialist, free-trade agitation in business, government and academic circles in the U.S. American and, indeed, foreign prosperity were seen to depend upon the free mobility of capital and goods across the globe. The United States officially supported the removal of tariffs and all trade barriers worldwide. The U.S. also worked for the free convertibility of currencies. Politically, the U.S. adopted a stance welcoming the independence of former colonial territories.

The international role of the dollar as it increasingly replaced the pound sterling as a reserve currency exemplified the hegemonic position of the U.S. Dollars accumulated abroad as reserves greatly facilitated continued capital exports by U.S. firms and continued military and economic programs abroad by the U.S. government. The acceptance by Europeans and Japanese of huge and rapidly accumulating dollar reserves is probably as good a measure as any of the hegemonic position of the United States.

Three consequences of the hegemonic position of the United States relate directly to the issue of world inequality. First, the more or less "free" expansion of multinational corporations marked a period of renewed intensive division of labor on a worldwide scale. Not unlike Britain after Napoleon (excepting, of course, much of the agricultural sector) the U.S. after World War II shifted "from the position of a net exporter of metals and minerals to that of a net importer" — a fact considered by the President's Commision on Foreign Economic Policy as "of overshadowing significance in shaping our foreign economic policies."[14] Further, the U.S. was increasing imports of "non-technology intensive" manufactured products far more rapidly than exports: after 1958, the U.S. became a growing net importer of such manufactures.[15] The United States was developing deepening lines of dependence on a worldwide division of labor in which U.S. exports were increasingly limited to high-technology manufactures (computers, airplanes, etc.) and food (also cotton and tobacco). In this context it is worth mentioning that by 1970, some 17 per cent of U.S. fruit production was exported, 33 per cent of the value of cotton and corn; 42 per cent of tobacco; and over 60 per cent of wheat and soybean outputs.[16]

The economic dependence of trade flows evolving under U.S. hegemony was matched by a growing dependence on earnings on foreign investments of U.S. firms and individuals. Such earnings rose from under 10 per cent of after-tax profits of domestic U.S. non-financial corporations in 1950 to nearly 22 per cent by 1965.[17] By 1967, it was estimated, the value of output associated with the international production of American-based multinationals amounted to $120 billion — a sum greater than the GNP of any capitalist nation excepting the U.S.[18]

The period of U.S. hegemony also witnessed the expansion of multinationals based in other nations, chiefly of Western Europe.[19] Complex webs of international trade and investment had developed quickly under U.S. hegemony.

The second consequence of U.S. hegemony to the late 1960's was the substitution of neo-colonialism for the old colonialism. The irreversibility of political independence meant that foreign aid replaced colonial administrators. And with foreign aid came foreign multinationals, often in direct proportion. Exports, imports and investments in the underdeveloped countries all grew, but far more slowly than such flows among the advanced capitalist nations. The motives of the multinationals, besides profit, included protecting existing market shares, securing via ownership the sources of internationally scarce inputs, etc. Quite some leeway existed for newly independent states to bargain with different multinationals for a "best deal". However, the costs of starting up a new independent government, the drain of profit outflows, left-over debts from pre-independence days, and/or costs of ambitious development projects could and usually did combine to produce serious, recurrent balance of payments difficulties. Recourse to the IMF or the U.S. — the two most likely sources of relief — rarely proved successful without implementation of "advice" to take internal austerity measures while further improving the climate for private foreign investments.

U.S. hegemony after World War II sharply constrained any independent or rapid economic development in most underdeveloped areas. Although independence in Asia and Africa gave more freedom of action to political and economic leaders, the international economy, the growth spurt of Western Europe and Japan and the hegemony of the U.S. meant that freedom could not lead to much. Indeed, what development did occur in the underdeveloped areas before the later 1960's had more to do with the weakness of imperial (or, in Latin America, U.S.) control during the Depression of the 1930's. It was then that national bourgeoisies in certain Latin American and Asian countries made real strides toward at least some small domestic manufacturing base (producing low-technology manufactures and rarely, if ever, intermediate or capital goods)[20] Those national bourgeoisies which had been able to develop before and during the 1930's were able to make some advances after 1945 as more state power fell into their hands. The widespread frustration with the lack of rapid economic development in the periphery reflected in part the relative disinterest of the multinationals whose focus was far more on the profits to be made in inter-advanced-capitalist trade and investment.

The third key consequence of post-1945 U.S. hegemony was the recovery of independent capitalist economies in Western Europe and Japan. Excepting the special case of England, the war-induced disruption of their economies left intact their populations' skills and buying habits and considerable quantities of plant and equipment. They needed capital. If it were forthcoming and would allow purchase of the latest types of efficient plant and equipment, rapid development might ensue. For reasons of U.S. hegemonic strategy, the capital necessary to get self-sustaining growth underway did arrive. European and Japanese growth accelerated, carving out special niches in manufacturing where competition against U.S.-based multinationals might prove successful. Alternative strategies were used: market sharing agreements and mergers were arranged. In general, specialisation of outputs proved to be the optimum oligopolistic strategy. Unlike Britain after 1846, Europe's officially promoted agriculture kept pace with demand. [21]

Reconstruction and specialisation in manufacturing, undertaken independently or in conjunction with U.S.-based multi-nationals, were the twin aspects of European and Japanese growth under post-war U.S. hegemony. This process left relatively minor room for interest or investment in the periphery; indeed, Japanese specialisation in high-efficiency, low-technology manufactures undermined, via exports, efforts to build similar industries in several underdeveloped countries. While there were, of course, exceptions to the simplified picture here sketched, nonetheless, I believe, the broad lines are correct. The conclusion: under the umbrella of U.S. hegemony, economic growth within and among Western Europe, Japan and the U.S. far outdistanced development in the periphery. World inequality grew, and not slowly. [22]

It was not that the periphery stagnated, although some parts certainly did. The periphery did experience at least periods of growth. The point, however, is that unchallenged hegemony exercised by one among the capitalist powers after 1945 operated so as to constrain development in the periphery even as it fostered rapid growth among the metropolitan centers. In this respect, despite many differing circumstances, U.S. hegemony after 1945 bears certain striking resemblances to British hegemony after Napoleon.

Serious capitalist challenges to U.S. hegemony emerged in the late 1960's following sporadic earlier rumblings. Simultaneously, full-scale war in Vietnam accelerated the developments challenging the continuation of U.S. hegemony. A rapidly maturing crisis among developed capitalist blocs brought far-reaching changes in their relations still underway at this time.

The fundamental issue was the economic revival of Western Europe and Japan which increasingly prompted corporate and political leaderships to critically review the costs and benefits of U.S. hegemony. To vastly oversimplify and condense a complex process, the strengthening of the European Common Market and severe weakening of the U.S. dollar reflected the conclusions being drawn in Europe and Japan about U.S. hegemony. Competition developed among three great capitalist centers: the U.S., the EEC (eventually absorbing EFTA) and Japan. U.S. hegemony began to erode. The competition and the erosion took place on two interacting levels: that of the multinational corporations and that of the three political groups seeking hegemony.

The strengthening of the EEC and the weakening of the dollar accelerated the rush of U.S.-based multinationals into Western European investments. This phenomenon was in turn linked to the rapid growth of the Euro-dollar market which accelerated the growth of the multinationals while freeing them more and more from various national authorities whose competitive strivings and occasional subservience to consumer and labor pressures rendered them more obstacles than aids to further growth. The uneven development during the period of U.S. hegemony undermined that hegemony not only on the level of the national state. Political competition carried over into competition of multinationals as, for example, multinationals based in different states, tried to exploit the advantages or compensate for the disadvantages that derived from the unevenly developing strength of those states.

The uncertainties of competition among hegemonic powers when compared with the earlier U.S. hegemony not only stimulated competition among multinationals, it also drove them to seek ever-greater independence from political authority.(23) But perhaps most importantly, in terms of international inequality, the new world environment led the multinationals to assign new attention, new resources and a new role to Third World territories in the international division of labor. However, before discussing this evolution further, a brief analysis of the breakdown of U.S. hegemony on the level of nation states (or groups) is warranted.

The enhanced relative economic and political power of Western Europe and Japan helped to revive protectionism and the old debate between protection and free trade among the capitalist powers. The three hegemonic groupings each sought the maximum freedom of manoeuver to accomplish both domestic prosperity and prosperity in their international economic dealings.

The mushrooming monetary crisis of the late 1960's and 1970's best exemplifies the forces at work.(24) In the Bretton Woods world of fixed exchange rates, basically no provision was made for sustained balance of payments imbalances. To put the same point differently, the hegemonic position of the U.S. was assumed permanent, hence no problem of a relative decline in the economic strength of the U.S. vis-à-vis the rest of the world was foreseen, and hence no real allowance for such an eventuality was built into the payments structure. Treaties and conventions among capitalist powers normally ignore the problem of uneven development; Bretton Woods and the IMF were no exception.

Thus as U.S. exports' competitiveness declined relatively, imports grew, especially from Europe and Japan, and the foreign costs of hegemony mounted reaching a crescendo with Vietnam. All the while, recovery and rapid growth in Europe attracted a flood of U.S. capital, mostly direct investment — this in itself a reflection of changing world power positions. All these factors combined to produce the regular, growing U.S. payments deficits of the 1950's, 1960's and 1970's. Before the late 1960's U.S. hegemony permitted U.S. deficits to function as reserve assets in foreign central banks, to provide the liquidity deemed essential to an expanding quantity of international trade. But reserve assets must be safe and secure, a requirement which the relative decline of the U.S. called increasingly into question. The full-blown crisis arrived at the end of the 1960's.

It was not solely because U.S. deficits mounted and U.S. gold reserves dwindled that Europe and Japan resisted further accumulation of increasingly unattractive dollar reserves. They also resisted because of pressure from firms based in their countries who understood that U.S. ability to run deficits was not unconnected with the ability of U.S.-based multinationals to invest freely abroad in ways competitive with and damaging to non-U.S. firms. Resistance to U.S. deficits was resistance to U.S. foreign investment was resistance to U.S. hegemony.

The August 15, 1971, declaration of President Nixon, cutting the U.S. free of the requirement to honor foreign dollar reserves with gold and devaluing the dollar, was the announcement of the end of a quarter-century of U.S. hegemony. Nothing I have seen since better sums up the situation then than the following journalistic account, written that same week:

> "What worries me most," says a Swiss economist, "is that there will be no action of any kind. We would then move into a generalized float — and that will be chaos." Ironically, the most helpful element in the whole picture is the memory that central bankers still have of the 1930's, when monetary cooperation disintegrated, the world moved into a generalized float, and there was chaos. No governmental official wants that to happen again.[25]

Precisely what the central bankers did not want and the governments did not want did in fact occur in the two and one half years since. The "dirty float" — a system of flexible exchange rates with admitted governmental interference to manipulate the float for national advantage — is a reality now and most likely will continue for some time.

The August, 1971, declaration also heralded open international competition among capitalist nations, more open than before. Rapid changes emerged in U.S., European and Japanese economic and political relations with all elements of the socialist bloc. The EEC and Japan accelerated efforts to establish wide-ranging special economic relationships with certain parts of the underdeveloped world: Japanese officials discussed a "yen settlement union" in Asia in January, 1972.[26] Western European and Japanese governments developed a variety of mechanisms to make dollar holdings available to firms in their countries on especially favorable terms. European and Japanese direct investment in the U.S. is beginning to acquire significant magnitude: witness the announcement of May 13, 1974, of a $1 billion German direct investment in the U.S. to build and assemble Volkswagens, the largest such investment in U.S. history. In return for newly opening up her economy to foreign investment, Japan is eagerly moving from a phase of manufacturing in which success came from undercutting U.S. firms to a phase of interlocking with those firms as an equal partner in domestic and foreign ventures — all with the political blessing of the U.S., for whom such ventures represent a current or potential outflanking of European competitors.[27]

In a world of competing hegemonic capitalisms, the competing multinationals face a more uncertain environment than that presided over by U.S. hegemony earlier. If, for example, the U.S. succeeds in shifting some of the military costs of protecting world capitalism onto Europeans and Japanese, the latter will acquire greater political influence over parts or all of the non-socialist world. Shifting political influences require shifting corporate decisions by multinationals.

Drawing upon the 1870-1913 period examined earlier and considering the special circumstances of post-1945 U.S. hegemony and its decline, I would present the following projection of what may be expected in the immediate future. The United States does not passively part with its hegemony. Competition among and between the U.S., the expanded EEC and Japan will intensify, which does not, of course, preclude certain times and places where competition itself calls forth temporary cooperation and alliances. Competition among multinationals will continue to intensify and continue to be both cause and effect of the competition among hegemonic powers. What Joan Robinson refers to as "begger-my-neighbor" policies of one capitalist power against another, each manipulating taxes, exchange rates, etc. against the others, will intensify. In these situations, multinationals based in each country will try to turn these policies toward their own advantage in competing with multinationals based elsewhere. In the words of one spokesman for U.S. multinationals:

> There is no question that production will flow from plants abroad; the question is who will own such plants. If U.S. interests connot compete abroad in running such plants as a result of a severe and untenable U.S. tax burden on such foreign operations, it is clear that the ownership of such plants will fall to others. This would not be in the best interests either of the United States or of American business at home or abroad.[28]

Within the capitalist mode of production, uncertainty has always had a cause and effect relationship with competition. Among hegemonic powers and multinational corporations increased competition and uncertainty reinforce each other. In this climate, multinationals will, I suspect, renew and change their interest in Third

World territories open to them. Competition among multinationals will point to the current and future importance of capturing Third World markets and real or potential sources of supply. This is no different from the 1870-1913 period. What promises to be different is the growing interest of multinationals in using Third World territories as sites for manufacturing consumer goods and an increasing quantity and variety of intermediate or capital goods. These are to be produced for the domestic market where the plants are located and for worldwide export in competition with other multinationals.

We may cite, here, only a very few items of evidence in support of such a trend. From one of the most authoritative publications in the Federal Republic of Germany comes a suggestive recent summary of the international economic situation. After noting the critical current importance of raw materials available abundantly in the developing countries, attention is drawn to the fact that developed countries "are dependent on exports. Socially, too, they are under the pressure of their own capacities." Then, perhaps the most interesting comment: "The developing countries have the raw materials, they have the potential labor forces, often they have even better locations than the industrial states. One cannot buy any of the three. Either one has them or one has not."[29] Further, consider these excerpts from a recent interview of Dr. Hans Leibkutsch, Chairman of the East Asia Association in Germany:

> The rise in costs in the Federal Republic of Germany is increasingly bringing industrial companies up against the alternatives... The move to other production centers appears to be the most realistic alternative. Export-oriented investments seem to have been increasing their share of the total of German foreign investment in this area in recent times.[30]

Another thorough recent report of economic conditions in Western Europe concludes that conditions for foreign direct investments there are markedly deteriorating.[31]

Implanting manufacturing facilities in Third World countries will involve some special difficulties for multinationals now. The at least nominal independence of these countries will require multinationals to compete for their loyalty. The indigenous bourgeoisies, where earlier lapses of imperial control permitted them to develop, will have to be at least partially accommodated as part of the competition for the necessary loyalty of Third World governments.[32] During the 1870-1913 period, such competition for the loyalties of political authorities in the pre-colonial territories (and this is also true of Latin America) soon eventuated in colonial annexation.[33] The question this leaves us with is: will the competition among multinationals result in producing a neo-colonial redivision of the Third World into three parts, each tightly connected, albeit "independent," with the U.S., the expanded EEC or Japan? Can we foresee three great transnational trading blocs comprising world capitalism?

And what about world inequality, and what about economic development in Third World countries, its quantity and quality? If the analysis here developed proves correct, we may expect some quite rapid industrialization in many parts of the Third World. The interaction of today's hegemonic powers will produce that. Multinationals will arrive in force bringing sizeable investments in manufacturing and the accoutrements of a foreign manufacturing establishment, i.e. investments in hotels, banking, tourist facilities, housing, wholesale and retail trade, etc. This image of the next phase of development in the periphery accords quite closely with that arrived at by Samir Amin and described by him as the "third stage in the development of peripheral capitalism," characterized by the production and export of cheaper manufactures offsetting the imports of food from the advanced capitalist countries as well as those capital goods and other manufactures which the advanced countries choose to specialize in.[34]

All this will produce economic development, viewed quantitatively. It will produce great changes in the class structure in Third World countries. Amin, for example, believes it will destroy the short-lived special privileges of whatever "aristocracy of labor" grew up in Third World economies before.[35] Yet the quality of this development will still be determined elsewhere, at the decision-making level of multinationals competitively manoeuvering among conflicting hegemonic powers. Shifting power positions among the hegemonic groupings will produce twists and turns, fits and starts in the development process in the Third World, which will also be subject to the extreme tensions resulting from rapid industrialization domestically. Once dependent on multinational firms for the maintenance of manufacturing employment and revenues, Third World governments will lose some of the little independence they have.

There will be development in the Third World, quite possibly rapid development. There was such development during the period of competing hegemonic powers after 1870. But now, as then, that development is subject to decision-making over which it has little, if any control. Now, as then, the development is dependent, subordinate, erratic and imbalanced. It is reasonable to suppose that development now, like development then, will build in economic patterns and rigidities that will impede adjustment of Third World economies to far-reaching economic or political changes in the advanced capitalist world. [36] It is, I believe, also reasonable to suppose that quantitatively and qualitatively industrialization in the capitalistically organized Third World will not change its relative inequality, political and economic, vis-à-vis the hegemonic capitalisms and the multinational corporations.

The fundamental alternative for overcoming the enduring posture of such relative inequality, the only available alternative, remains socialist revolution and socialist development. Socialism thus remains on the immediate agenda of the people of the Third World. And the immediate future must necessarily reflect this fact.

NOTES

(1) See, for example, A. L. Levine, *Industrial Retardation in Britain, 1880-1914* (New York: Basic Books, 1967); D.H. Aldcroft, editor, *The Development of British Industry and Foreign Competition, 1875-1914* (London: Allen and Unwin, 1968); and D.C.M. Platt, "Economic Factors in British Policy During the 'New Imperialism'," *Past and Present* 39 (April, 1968), pp. 120-138, to name just a few of the major works.
(2) R.D. Wolff, *The Economics of Colonialism: Britain and Kenya, 1870-1930* (New Haven: Yale University Press, 1974), pp. 1-29.
(3) See L.H. Jenks, *The Migration of British Capital to 1875* (New York, Knopf, 1927) and H. Feis, *Europe, the World's Banker* (New Haven: Yale University Press, 1930).
(4) The reasons why capitalists and capitalist states strive necessarily and incessantly for hegemony and the imperialism implied by that hegemony are not the focus of this paper. They are, in any case, adequately summarized in V.I. Lenin, *Imperialism, the Highest Stage of Capitalism* (Moscow: Foreign Languages Publishing House, 1959); H. Magdoff, *The Age of Imperialism* (New York: Monthly Review, 1969); and R.D. Wolff, "Modern Imperialism: the View from the Metropolis," *American Economic Review: Papers and Proceedings* (May, 1970).
(5) Cf. Wolff, *Economics of Colonialism, passim.*
(6) Karl Marx, *Capital* (Moscow: Foreign Languages Publishing House, 1959), 1: 451. See also Marx and F. Engels, *On Colonialism* (Moscow: Foreign Languages Publishing House, n.d.).
(7) See Lenin, *op. cit.*
(8) "Semi-colonies" refers chiefly to Latin America.
(9) See Gabriel Kolko, *The Politics of War, the World, and United States Foreign Policy, 1943-1945* (New York: Random House, 1969); and Joyce and Gabriel Kolko, *The Limits of Power, the World and United States Foreign Policy, 1945-1954* (New York: Harper and Row, 1972).
(10) See Magdoff, *op. cit.*, pp. 54-62. This entire work presents abundant data on the U.S. hegemonic period.

(11)   C.P. Kindleberger, *American Business Abroad* (New Haven: Yale University Press, 1969), p. 45.
(12)   *Ibid.,* pp. 129-130. Kindleberger shows comparably high rates earned in Australia and India.
(13)   P.B. Kenen, *Giant Among Nations* (Chicago: Rand, McNally, 1963), pp. 149-152, 161-162. If U.S. military aid to Western Europe is added, the total flow grows from $25 to $34 billion.
(14)   Commission on Foreign Economic Policy, *Staff Papers Presented to the Commission,* Washington, February, 1954, p. 224, quoted in Magdoff, *op. cit.,* p. 49.
(15)   P.G. Peterson, *The United States in the Changing World Economy,* vol. 2: Statistical Background Material, Washington, December, 1971, Charts 19, 20 and 21. This official report was prepared for the President and the Council on International Economic Policy during 1971.
(16)   *Ibid.,* vol. 2, p. 14.
(17)   Magdoff, *op. cit.,* p. 183.
(18)   J. Polk, "The New World Economy," *Columbia Journal of World Business* (January-February, 1968), quoted in S. Rolfe, *The International Corporation: A Background Report for the 22nd Congress of the International Chamber of Commerce* (Istanbul: The Congress, May-June, 1969), pp. 8-9. For detailed data, by firm, on the shares of foreign assets, sales and profits totals in the period 1965-67, see Rolfe, *op. cit.,* pp. 150-153.
(19)   *Ibid.,* Tables 5, 16, 17, 18a and 19.
(20)   Cf. the analysis of Brazil in A.G. Frank, *Capitalism and Underdevelopment in Latin America* (New York: Monthly Review Press, 1967), pp. 177ff.
(21)   European agriculture was carefully protected and developed after 1945. By the early 1960's, Western European countries were able to produce 95% of their grain consumption and 100% of their consumption of potatoes, sugar, vegetables, pork, cheese and butter. There were serious thoughts given to European exports of such items. See M.M. Postan, *An Economic History of Western Europe, 1945-1964* (London: Methuen, 1967), p. 178. All the while labor was flowing from agriculture to industry in Europe at a rapid pace: see *Ibid.,* p. 191. All this left little role for much development in the periphery. The picture of post-1945 agricultural development in Japan is more mixed: see J. Halliday and G. McCormack, *Japanese Imperialism Today* (New York: Monthly Review Press, 1973), pp. 170-178.
(22)   The 1950's and 1960's were years of lament over the grim future foreseen for development in the aspiring Third World — complaints regarding terms of trade, enclaves, synthetics replacing natural materials, etc. The relative weight in world trade of Third World exports and imports fell sharply in magnitude, if not in the continuing essential role they played for economic health in the developed capitalist world. See P. Jalee, *The Third World in World Economy* (New York: Monthly Review Press, 1969), pp. 77-90. The interpretation of these facts suggested by the discussion in this paper is that U.S. hegemony more than any fact of production or consumption patterns among the developed countries explains the relative decline of the periphery with its consequences for development there.
(23)   National objectives of states simply differed from the international objectives of the multinationals. Cf. Kindleberger, *op. cit.,* pp. 140-144. For an interesting argument that the growth of multinationals weakened state power in the advanced capitalist powers through the continual conflict between national and multinational firms to control policy, see G. Junne, "Internationalization of Economic Processes and Fulfillment of State Functions," *Kapitalistaat* 2 (1973), p. 52.
(24)   See Magdoff, *op. cit.,* pp. 67-114; and also P. Sweezy and H. Magdoff, *The Dynamics of U.S. Capitalism* (New York: Monthly Review Press, 1972), pp. 149-212 (these are reprints of articles that appeared earlier in *Monthly Review*).
(25)   *Business Week* (August 21, 1971), p. 27, quoted in Sweezy and Magdoff, *op. cit.,* p. 209.
(26)   Halliday and McCormack, *op. cit.,* pp. 219ff.
(27)   Cf. the discussion of joint U.S.-Japanese automobile manufacturing ventures in the *Wall-Street Journal,* May 7 and 8, 1974.
(28)   U.S. Council for the International Chamber of Commerce, *Summary of Statement by William J. Nolan, Jr., Chairman of the Committee on Taxation of the Council, before the Ways and Means Committee, House of Representatives, March 15, 1973* (New York: the Council, n.d.).
(29)   M. Timmler, "Die Explosion der Entwicklungslander," *Aussenpolitik* 25 (1. Quartal, 1974), pp. 80-92 (Translated by F.A. Bishop and A. Tait).
(30)   See *Ubersee Rundschau,* No 2, Vol. 26 (March, 1974), p. VI.

(31) For an extensive 100 pages of evidence, carefully sifted, documenting growing difficulties for U.S. investors intending to move into or remain in Western Europe, see J.J. Boddewyn, "Western European Policies Toward U.S. Investors," *The Bulletin* (Published by the New York University Graduate School of Business Administration Institute of Finance), No. s 93-95 (March, 1974). The difficulties discussed are: slower and more erratic growth, inflation, burgeoning costs, growing state interventionism, growing labor militancy of various types, environmental concerns, and "an attack against capitalism in general."

(32) See the excellent discussion and demonstration of these tendencies at work in Latin America in F.H. Cardoso, "Dependency and Development in Latin America, "*New Left Review* 74 (July-August, 1972), pp. 83-95; and J. Wells, "Recent Developments in Brazilian Capitalism," *Bulletin of the Conference of Socialist Economists* (Winter, 1973), pp. 1-12.

(33) Cf. Wolff, *Economics of Colonialism*, pp. 30-46.

(34) See the summary of this view presented in Samir Amin, "Review of G. Arrighi and J.S. Saul, *Essays on the Political Economy of Africa,*" *Monthly Review* 25 (October, 1973), pp. 52-57.

(35) *Ibid.*

(36) See the interesting focus on this aspect of the long-term costs of dependent development in Tamas Szentes, *The Political Economy of Underdevelopment* (Budapest: Akademiai, 1973), pp. 133-165.

ECONOMIC DEVELOPMENT IN THE DEPENDENT WORLD

Mohamed Dowidar

What are the real possibilities for economic development in dependent countries?

We shall begin with the basic economic realities[1] of these societies which may be said to be characterized by an effort to grow, a so-called strategy of import substitution. We shall use this latter term, as it is widely accepted even if it lacks scientific foundation. One cannot really define a strategy by simply enunciating the areas of economic activity which will be given priority in economic policy. A strategy is defined by its class structure. This is why we prefer to talk, for these societies, about the strategy of alliance between the middle classes and the petty bourgeoisie. This enables us to see the strategy of "import-substitution" from the perspective of both the direct producers[2] and international capital.

We shall examine closely the types of social-political regimes which use this strategy in today's world economy in order to analyze their limitations in terms of solving the national problem as well as the socio-economic problems of direct producers. This will enable us to specify the domains of social activity wherein lie the real possibilities of economic development.

On the basis of these facts, we shall consider alternative strategies for real socio-economic development, and describe its general characteristics.

In the world process of development and under-development, import-substitution as a growth strategy appeared at a certain stage of the development of the capitalist world-economy. At first it was a limited process, becoming a significant phenomenon in the 1930's, but one which had already manifested itself earlier in Latin American countries[3], in Egypt and, indeed, in India. Later on, it occurs in the framework of deliberate attempts by under-developed countries in the period following World War II, after gaining their political independence.

Let us look now, without going into details, at how import-substitution manifested itself during both periods. During the first, colonization of these countries led, in the subsequent phase, to their integration in the world capitalist market. This integration was brought about by a continuous process of the primitive accumulation of capital in these countries. Capital penetrated these countries, displacing former modes of production, modifying some of their main characteristics, creating a supply of labor for the market. It was also marked by the appearance, within the framework of foreign capital, of some local capital (often termed national capital, but I do not think this correct.) This state of affairs was created by the orientation of the economy as a whole towards external trade. The dynamism of the economy thus depended on the demand for export products.

With World War I and the Great Depression of the 1930's, many factors permit the establishment of some industries in under-developed countries.

The Great Depression, reflecting a deep crisis in capitalism, and the World War, a conflict between national capitals, weakened the grip of metropolitan capital on under-developed societies. This created the possibility — indeed, during the War when local markets were isolated, the necessity — for foreign or local capital to move into new production sectors. It also provided the occasion to establish customs and tariff barriers to protect the new productive activities. This was the case at least for Egypt, where the threat of Japanese dumping of textiles during the Depression years contributed to the establishing of such a system of tariff protection.

The War and the Depression had a strong influence on export patterns. Exports declined in volume and prices fell disastrously (within the framework of a long-term trend characterized by a fall in the demand for primary products and a worsening of the terms of trade.) Together they reduced the import capacity of under-developed economies, thus announcing the end of a period when exports were the main growth factor for these economies. Without import capacity, some solution by substitution had to be devised.

The local production of these goods turned out to be profitable for the capital controlling the economy. For, on the one hand, there was already local demand for such goods resulting both from distribution of incomes and consumption patterns derived from previous imports. On the other hand, as far as supply was concerned, the profitability of producing these goods was guaranteed: by the existence on the market of a relatively cheap supply of manpower which could be employed, even with limited technical training, to produce industrial consumption goods (textiles, food products, etc.). This supply of labour came from two sources: the flow of workers from the countryside as a consequence of the continuous process of primitive capital accumulation, and the increase of the labor force due to natural population growth; by the existence of a certain infrastructure for basic services (even if these were essentially established to meet the needs of an economy oriented foreign trade.)

This series of factors led to the creation of some industries whose products would substitute for imports. The substitution model is thus determined by the set of imported goods and is characterised by: simplified technology, thus implying a limited reliance on imports of machinery, and the availability of local primary inputs required for production. Such a model resulted in decreased pressures on the balance of payments, but in an enhanced dependence of the economy as a whole. This dependency manifests itself; in dependence on exports which continued to be distributed in the capitalist centres; in a consumption model which is basically defined and developed via the trade relations with capitalist core countries; in dependence on machinery, i.e. technological dependence.

What are the results of such a strategy from the point of view of regional disparities within the under-developed economy? Since conditions favourable to import substitution industries were optimum in urban areas, regional disparities were bound to increase between urban areas (whose social structure is far from being homogenous) and rural areas (where the social structure also lacks homogeneity.)

In every case, this phase of import substitution represents, for these countries, participation in a new form of international capitalist division of labour.

The second period starts with the era of national liberation movements in the colonies, and with national political independence (sometimes real, but more often than not purely formal.) Import substitution was adopted as the growth strategy, but implemented this time in the following manner: increased state intervention; in some cases, growth efforts come only from the state (the state sector); in other cases, the state and private capital combine their efforts. In a third category of countries, foreign capital still plays a major role. In some cases, it dominates the market, making it extremely difficult for local capital to establish itself; capital-intensive techniques are used, thus reducing employment levels in these countries and implying a further strong demand for imported production goods.

In this case, what has resulted is the establishment of some imports substitution industries (I shall refrain from calling it industrialization), which has not necessarily lessened pressures on the balance of payments: insofar as this substitution has not affected the imports of luxury consumption goods; because, the necessary primary inputs to construct such industries have not been readily available within the country, and the consumer durables industries have often had to import the semi-finished products they needed. The effect on the balance of payments situation was probably negative. Before the establishment of these industries, it was still possible, in times of balance of payments difficulties, to reduce imports of finished products and to lessen foreign debts. Once these industries were installed and employed a part of the active labour force, the import function became inelastic, even in times of balance of payment difficulties, because of the negative political and employment consequences of any cutback on output.

Imports are substituted, but within a framework of general dependency for the economy as a whole. This dependency is double and it involves: a pattern of consumption which is not only a creation of the recent past, but is also constantly behind that of advanced capitalist economies. The most dangerous consequence of this policy is that it perpetuates the present consumption pattern in accordance with the present value system it embodies, distracting attention from the fact that the value system must also change if society is to develop; a pattern of exports which remains essentially that of primary products without excluding, however, at this stage, some industrial exports. As far as the products of import substitution industries are concerned, they are difficult to export abroad since they are in the main similar to those produced in other under-developed countries.

This general dependency of under-developed economies results from the overwhelming presence of monopolies on the world market, or from the non-competitiveness of these products in quality terms, or from a combination of these two factors.

Continued import of basic production goods and semi-finished goods, also implies technological dependency. In terms of regional disparities, this strategy results in a concentration of these industries in existing urban areas, and as a consequence, the reproduction, at a qualitatively larger scale, of the colonial model of regional disparities. However, a new element in the rural-urban relationship is introduced as local capital replaces foreign capital, the terms of trade between agricultural and non-agricultural products are unfavourable for the countryside. The post-independence cities replace the former capitalist metropolis in the extortion of a part of the agricultural surplus.

Since the linkage-effects of established industries occur abroad, somewhere in the core capitalist countries, the centers of development continue to exist outside of the dependent economy. What were supposed to become "growth poles" are mere transmission points for the real centre located in some advanced capitalist economy. Such cities have a specific function: they do not supply the countryside with what true centres provide to agriculture, even in capitalist societies. They live on the appropriation of part of the surplus created through primary production and by the few existing industries. How large this part is depends on their bargaining power in international capitalist markets. They facilitate the extraction of the rest of the surplus by the capitalist core countries, although not always without some resistance.

In these post-independence cities, two groups live: on the one hand, the dominant social class or stratum, the so-called elite, with its own life-style, its consumption patterns, its ideals, etc, and, on the other hand, the lower classes of the urban population, whose living conditions are worsening and whose numbers are increasing because of a deteriorating situation in the countryside and a relaxation on population movement after independence.

This is what the strategy of import substitution looks like in the reality of the world process of development and under-development. As such, it corresponds to one of the phases of capitalist strategy, a strategy that changes as the structure of the capitalist system evolves. In other words, the strategy of capital[4] on the world market is not eternally given. It evolves in response to structural changes, both in the developed and in the under-developed parts of the capitalist world-economy. The international capitalist division of labour has a dynamic of its own. As the capitalist mode of production evolves, its form changes. We can distinguish the following phases:

In the first phase of capitalist industrialization, the emphasis is laid on consumption industries. Peripheral countries (colonies), having been forced to pay tribute during the previous phase of the accumulation of money-capital, are required to supply primary products and to constitute a market for industrial products.

Once specialization has taken place in the industries of the capitalist core countries, and emphasis has shifted towards basic industries, the (colonial) periphery is required to produce (new) primary materials and food products, and to continue to serve as market outlets.

With the construction of a strong industrial base in the centre, capital reproduces itself at a quantitatively different scale in order to alter the relations of production in the colonies (integration and transformation of the colonies), directly incorporating the labour force thus created and subordinating the modes of production prevailing in rural societies. This process also entails the possibility of the emergence of some local capital within the framework of foreign capital.

Once there is the development of basic industries in the core countries and local capital in dependent societies, a crisis or a general war might, for a time, weaken the control of metropolitan capital on the dependent society, opening the way, but not without difficulty, to local production of industrial consumption goods. Some substitution of imported commodities would occur. In addition to primary inputs and agricultural products, the dependent society would then be in a position to produce some consumer goods. However, in the core countries basic industries would already have become relatively stronger. This is thus simply a change in the form of the international capitalist division of labour.

The present phase is characterized, within core capitalist countries, by the development of new and impressive industries of the means of production, and on the international scene, by the existence of countries which are striving to establish a socialist society, and of national liberation movements in colonies and the creation of new states in former colonies. Politically-independent underdeveloped countries may at that stage attempt to produce, in addition to primary materials (e.g. oil) and agricultural products, some industrial consumer goods and even certain traditional production goods such as cement, steel, etc. This would be achieved through import substitution policies and could represent a new departure in the international capitalist division of labour.

It is in this stage we find ourselves. It is therefore of primary importance to analyze what may be the general strategy of international capital (including conflicts between various national groupings) to maintain the state of dependency of the under-developed economies in perhaps a new form. This strategy might involve coming to terms with the under-developed countries, and would develop into the transformation of the economic activities of underdeveloped countries as previously suggested; changes in the production patterns of advanced capitalist economies; a decrease in the expansion rate of traditional consumer-goods industries and a rapid growth of new key-sectors (petro-chemicals, electronics, etc.); a crisis in the export sector in under-developed countries. All these could result in some form of specialization for under-developed economies in the production of traditional industrial consumer goods (textiles, food products, etc.); some production of some consumer durables, as well as the production of some traditional heavy industry.

This new form of specialization does not eliminate the dependency of under-developed economies vis-à-vis core capitalist countries (who will concentrate on new key branches of production) and therefore technological dependency will continue.

In terms of employment, the new strategy of international capital will tend to a situation whereby migration of highly skilled labour towards capitalist centres would continue and since an important part of the surplus produced in the under-developed economies is drained out and since another part of this surplus fills the consumption needs of dominant classes in the under-developed economy (given its mode of distribution of income), this latter part being devoted to the purchase of consumer goods as determined by the centre, the growth rate of the under-developed economy will remain limited. If we add to this the tendency in under-developed economies to establish capital-intensive industrial projects, manpower absorptive capacity in the new industries will be limited. Consequently, there will continue to be a labour surplus within the agricultural production units, whose social form is the family, and any increase in manpower will join the ranks of the industrial reserve army packed in urban areas. This labour force could be utilized either by an exodus (relatively limited) of this labour force from under-developed societies to capitalist societies, or by the movement of capital (which by contrast is highly mobile) into the under-developed economies.

At the socio-political level, I believe the new strategy of international capital involves either the maintenance or the creation in an under-developed economy of a situation characterized by a transfer of effective control of the means of production (if it is not already controlled capital from the core countries) as well as a transfer of political power from the old ruling classes to the middle class and the petty bourgeoisie. In fact, one should seriously study the social and ideological affiliations of these latter classes, as well as their ideals and life-styles (usually geared abroad). Political power tends to lie with new "neutral" groups who live on the appropriated surplus without contributing anything to the social process of work and who are in direct opposition to direct producers.

It appears that when international capital does not intervene directly in countries with an under-developed economy, it tends to prefer to deal with states that have a "public sector". Why?

For reasons of efficiency. International capital takes the form of large corporations. As far as they are concerned, it is preferable to negotiate contracts with large units within under-developed economies, with the state. After all, very few under-developed countries have a volume of activities superior to that of General Motors.

Even when natural resources (copper, oil, etc.) are produced by state enterprises, the process of transformation and their distribution on international markets are generally taken care of by companies in the hands of international capital. Capitalist enterprises can thus control the share of profit appropriated by state companies in under-developed countries.

The fact that the state owns the firms places it between international capital and the national workers of the enterprises. Thus, international capital avoids direct conflicts with workers.

State nationalization of some companies gives the state some international political support which it may greatly need to survive. It also gives it more bargaining power in its dealing with international capital as they jointly share the economic surplus produced by the under-developed economy.

The State has thus a vital importance in the under-developed society. One has to define its socio-political nature and its role. This analysis can only be made on the basis of knowledge of the social stratification of the particular society.

One can readily understand that the strategy of import substitution is in fact the strategy of international capital in the present phase of development of the international capitalist economy. It can be used in under-developed economies, thus creating a new form of the division of labour but one in keeping with the norms of capitalist markets, i.e. within the framework of dependency and under-development.

This strategy is carried out in most dependent societies, the form varying, sometimes significantly, according to the concrete historical background, by socio-political regimes which act inside their societies in the context of the world-economy. To consider what are the real possibilities for economic development, we will have to examine more closely the types of regimes and the general characteristics of the world-economy. Let us start with the world-economy considered as an organic entity composed of heterogeneous parts, among which one can distinguish advanced capitalist sectors, under-developed sectors with capitalist relations of production, sectors experiencing the difficulties of a transition in the direction of a socialist society,[5] difficulties both internal and external. The study of the two parts of the international capitalist economy should be centered around the relationship of labor and capital in the advanced and under-developed sectors in order to define the specific factors in each sector and assess the state of the class struggle in the two parts of the capitalist world.

While we are dealing with an organically unified totality, we shall try to explain the situation in terms of what happens in dependent countries.

In these societies, capital manifests itself in relationship to direct producers in two ways: The first case is those units of production where capital exists both as a social phenomenon and as individual shares of capital acting within the production unit itself. We have in this case capitalist units of production based upon wage-labour whose *surplus-value* is appropriated by local and international capital. The second case is where capital is exclusively a social phenomenon without being present within production units. We have then *family units* which still produce agricultural or handicraft products through the work of *members of the family*. They sometimes experience qualitative changes because of the exchange relationships in which they are involved as purchasers of inputs necessary for their production or of consumption goods including food, or when they sell their products on the internal or on the international market. It is through these exchange relationships that capital, as the dominant social phenomenon, appropriates the *surplus* product of these family units. This is one of the specific traits of a dependent society, and which determines how such a social whole functions within the international capitalist market. These production units acquire a particular importance since they supply relatively inexpensive food to direct producers both in the country and the city. Thus the entire level of wages of the dependent society can be kept fairly low. The existence of these family units, especially in agriculture, makes it extremely difficult to organize direct producers, thereby weakening the struggle against local and international capital.

There are thus two large classes of direct producers: peasants and workers, each containing within it different strata: varying size of plots for small independent peasants or tenants, agricultural and industrial workers integrated or not in the process of production, etc. Overall, these are the classes (present or potential) that produce surplus in the various domains of economic activity.

Opposed to them, one finds the owners of the means of production in the towns or in the country, with their own internal social stratification, and with potential contradictions both among these classes whether in the country or in the towns, as well as between the towns and the rural areas.

Earlier we demonstrated how local capital developed within foreign capital and how it attempted in times of crises (economic or military) to extend its domination over local production at a time when direct producers did not yet represent an alternative social and political force. They did not thus yet represent a direct threat to capital. This threat only materialized as direct producers became conscious of their situation and organized themselves, politically and in trade-unions. As the threat grew bigger, local capital withdrew in favour of international capital, bringing us to *the present situation* where it accepts some form or other of subordination to international capital. We are coming to the point where the main contradiction will be the one existing between direct producers of economic surplus on the one hand and, on the other, local and international capital who appropriate it. The intensity of the latter contradiction and its manifestations depend on the degree of trade-union and political solidarity of direct producers. The more advanced their organization, the less acute is the contradiction between local and international capital. Finally the two enter into a tacit alliance, occasionally even an explicit one.

It is against this background that the social-political nature of the local state must be considered, as it develops during the colonial phase and, more importantly, after independence, which is often a mere formality.

Such political independence was often the end result of a revolutionary wave, resulting from the struggles of direct producers, or disputes between local and international capital. Perceiving this thrust which could not be resisted initially is essential to understand the politics of the local states, of the political institutions of regimes in dependent societies.

In the life-span of these regimes one can distinguish, roughly, first, a general axis along which their role is defined, and then, two phases of their existence.

The axis which characterizes their existence is the continuous struggle (with varying densities over time) against the forces of direct producers at all levels, economic, organizational, ideological. However, this struggle does not mean that direct producers do not succeed in wresting some gains in all three fields. It is in this light that one can understand the politics of these regimes in all fields of life.

As to the phases of the life-span of these regimes, there are two: the phase of establishing the regime, or what we might call, in terms of political sociology, the Bonapartist phase of the regime, and the phase of maintenance of the regime, once established. We shall examine the behavior of these regimes in both phases.

These regimes have emerged at a time when the United States, as the policeman of international capitalism, during the massive retaliation phase of nuclear strategy, showed indecisiveness in dealing with new regimes in the under-developed areas of the capitalist world: sometimes antagonistic, at times passive and often hesitant. The Soviet Union, guided by wrong theory, in fact limited by its own internal formation and by the nature of its State (created in a first phase) and by its own global interests (crystallized in a second phase), supported these new regimes even when they were oppressing the forces of the direct producers. This support furthermore was not accepted unquestioningly. The regimes were opportunistic. They embarked on a policy of tactical friendship with the U.S.S.R. They threatened the interests of former colonial powers, at least those who maintained their traditional style (one has to remember that these regimes took power following a revolutionary wave.) Towards the United States, the attitudes of these regimes still vacillated, but it never really threatened the basic interests of the United States.

At the level of ideology, these regimes were objectively anti-socialist, except that some lip service to socialist ideals had to be paid to appease direct producers. They embraced capitalist ideology, but in objective subordination as determined by the life-style of the dominant classes, by their interests as opposed to those of direct producers, and by their systems of values. They embraced it except insofar as it was against their interests in their conflict with international capital about the sharing of the surplus produced by direct producers at a time when the latter did not represent, in organizational terms, a threat to the interests of local capital (whether private or public.) During this phase, the State inevitably adopted measures adverse to the interests of former dominant classes in order to reduce their status. Thus, at the later state of alliance between these two groups, the new classes would be clearly the dominant partner.

During the second phase, the United States adopted an attitude which fulfilled the dynamic needs of world society and its structural changes. Their policy was to strike down violently, with all available means, the forces of direct producers in Third World societies with the exception, of course, of those cases where direct producers could fight back and eventually defeat imperialism. U.S. policy towards the regimes of these societies was to support, in varying degrees, those regimes which, given the recurring threat of the direct producers, especially in cases where the regimes were incapable of solving the immediate economic problems of their societies, accepted the imperialist presence led by the U.S. Thus comes the stage where these regimes accepted subordination to imperialist forces, a subordination which safeguarded the interests of local capital. The degree of subservience varied, from total subordination to secondary partnership as a sub-imperialist power.

During this stage, regimes relinquished their policy of tactical friendship with the U.S.S.R. while maintaining some form of contacts, as a hedge against possible "betrayal" by international capital. One has to bear in mind that, in economic terms, the Soviet Union remains a less effective partner in terms of product quality and variety, especially for those commodities needed to achieve the consumption pattern desired by the dominant classes. In all cases, the relinquishing of this "friendship" did not go beyond permissible limits as defined, for instance, by the policy of "peaceful coexistence" between the U.S. and the U.S.S.R., at least during the period when the problem of the modality of the imperial presence was not completely solved.

It is at this point we can speak of a "strategic" return (objectively at least, despite the subjective indecisiveness) to open alliance with international capital under some form of subordination, the acceptance of an imperialist presence, either direct or indirect. This alliance is linked to dreams of affluence within the bosom of international capital which in turn was to be granted all facilities to exploit internal resources after a "regrettable" absence. In fact, during the presumed absence, international capital never ceased to control the strategic resources of these countries (oil, metals, etc.). We can talk about "dreams," for in no way is their realization sure, even though they guarantee control over the direct producers. For capital has a rationality which subservient regimes do not usually comprehend and which may very well impose limits to their dreams. Let us take

Egypt for example. With a heritage of civilization which gives to its direct producers an extraordinary capacity for resistance (both passive and positive), with a considerable cultural as well as demographic weight in the Arab world, and with all that implies in terms of possibilities, which in a dynamic evolving situation (characterized by an unresolved national question, the constant hardship for direct producers of the high cost of living and unequal fiscal policy), can be transformed into arms in the hands of direct producers threatening local and foreign capital. In such a situation, one can assume that the rationality of international capital would impose limits to this options. It can only act within a framework where direct producers do not represent a threat with which Egypt could blackmail international capital's interests in the whole Arab world. These limits vary, of course, and always in terms of the rationality of capital, from one country to another. One can say that, in general, the less the economic and cultural weight of a country within an area, the greater these limits will be on the local regimes.

At the level of ideology, these regimes begin to adopt capitalism openly, but always in subordination. The slogans of the revolutionary days, which had been needed to win over direct producers, are dropped. Ideological arguments with classes in power before the Bonapartist era are forgotten, provided the new classes maintain some measure of supremacy and succeed in eliminating the opposition forces, through a systematic process of depoliticization of the masses, a process which is in fact intended to eliminate systematically any awareness of public issues which could threaten the state monopoly on their definition.

This is the situation which leaves unresolved both the national question and the social-economic problems of direct producers. The fact that the main contradiction occurs between direct producers (with their different strata) and international capital (local capital being aligned) shows that the national question and the social question are no longer separate: the mobilization of direct producers is based on a conscious national sentiment and on their relative consciousness of economic and social changes; the limited, indeed negative, role of local capital is revealed in its private or state form through the alliance of the middle classes and the petite bourgeoisie.

This leads us to conclude that the real possibilities for social-economic development in dependent societies is to be found in the struggle for national liberation waged by direct producers to get rid of all sort of subservience to local and/or international capital, the struggle to create the state dominated by the direct producers, sine qua non of their socio-economic development.

It is on this basis that one can envisage an alternative strategy for the socio-economic development of dependent countries.

In defining such an alternative strategy (development through structural transformation), we can only offer the outlines of a general scheme, given the varying conditions — both natural and social — of one under-developed society from another. One cannot forget that it is up to the society itself to make the final decision on the path to follow, a decision which in real life is collective. Thus we shall clearly limit ourselves to a general framework for the discussion of the various (important) general problems of social and economic under-development implied by the expression, strategy of development.

Given the class structure of society, any strategy poses the question: development by whom? and for whom? Let us be clear from the outset: we imply development of the majority, i.e., the masses of direct producers involved in agriculture and in other economic activities.

Development thus intends to satisfy *internal needs, the needs of the mass of direct producers*, and it can be achieved through structural changes in the organization and the forces of production as well as through the accumulation of the means of production. This definition raises two problems: the relationship between accumulation and consumption, and the definition of a consumption pattern for the masses.

Regarding the relationship between accumulation and consumption, from past historical experience, there appears to be two possible types of relationships:

In the capitalist model of development, capital accumulation is a goal per se as it forms the basis of social (as well as political) power and prestige. This accumulation process manifested itself initially in consumption products for which a demand existed, and later on in production goods. The ensuing consumption pattern corresponded to the pattern of income-distribution, as it had been created and maintained in the present phase of monopolistic manipulation of the market. (As far as consumption is concerned, the result is obtained through advertising and its subsequent costs.)

In the Soviet development experience, capital accumulation was taken as the goal in the initial phase of planned development. During this process of accumulation, priority was given to heavy industries as they existed in the Western world. Consumption (like agriculture) was considered a non-priority area, as residual. The fact that it was the same type of heavy industries already known in capitalist economies and that the consumption pattern chosen was also the one prevailing in urban societies resulted, at the end of the first phase of development, in a consumption pattern similar to the pattern prevailing in western capitalist economies.

Is it possible to envisage, in the light of these past experiences, a different type of relationship between accumulation and consumption, in which accumulation (both the quantity and the means) would be determined according to a specified consumption pattern? I believe the answer is yes. It is from this perspective at least that we shall elaborate an alternative development strategy.

We then must start by defining the consumption pattern to be achieved in the long run by and for the masses of direct producers. This will then constitute the *principal objective* of economic development. How may we define this consumption pattern?

The consumption pattern may be defined: on the basis of the present consumption pattern of direct producers, and on the basis of some concept of social needs (as opposed to individual needs), i.e., the needs of the masses which might be satisfied, given on the one hand their present standard of living, and on the other the available resources of society.

To define this consumption pattern, on all aspects of society's value-system ought also to be defined. The definition of the long-run consumption pattern of the masses implies knowing the resources available to the society.

A profound knowledge of these (potential) resources is essential for the elaboration and achievement of an alternative development strategy. Serious efforts should be devoted to evaluating the geological and other potentialities of each country.

Research should be conducted, on the basis of accumulated technological and scientific knowledge, to study the various technologies applied in other countries as well as authentic indigenous techniques, in order to discover among foreign techniques, those which could be adopted with or without modification, and among internal techniques, those which could be applied immediately without any change, those which would require some change, and those new techniques which would need to be devised.

Once the main objective, the mode of consumption of direct producers has been defined on the one hand, and the resources and technological possibilities inventoried on the other, this objective will be achieved by means of accumulation, which in turn will have been determined on the basis of the consumption pattern. In other words, it is on the basis of the consumption pattern that the level and pattern of accumulation (i.e. allocation of resources between various activities, the technical component of activities and their location) are defined.

But this definition of accumulation presumes:

A new concept of decision-making and new criteria on which to make them. Decisions will be taken by direct producers according to criteria of collective rationality, rather than on individualistic or bureaucratic criteria.

A different concept of the relation between agriculture and industry, one that seeks to abolish the contradiction between town and country, which can only be done through an appreciation of the complementarity of the two activities, and of others, outside of *market relations*, that is, by joining together to satisfy directly the needs of direct producers.

In the light of this different concept, one can consider in a new way the issue of choosing a technology and geographical location of industries, by recognizing that technology is not neutral. (Technology is only the means to achieve objectives which themselves reflect the interests of different classes and social strata.)

Finally, this definition of accumulation would be based upon a new concept of the division of labour within the social production unit. This division would reflect socialist production relationships, eliminating the contradiction between manual and intellectual workers, between the supervisor and the supervised, between men and women.

A process of accumulation thus defined is a process of structural changes and includes: changes in the income distribution pattern in favour of the masses. This transformation would be brought about through a new system of production relationship that would make possible: the elimination of foreign capital; the liberation of the economic surplus from those local classes who waste it in one way or another; finding new forms of organization for production units, forms which emerge from the concrete conditions of each society and which will turn out to foster development.

It also includes changes in the level of the productive forces within a society, that is changes whose objective is to increase productivity of the work force in the process of production and reproduction by the *liberation of the creative energies of the active population* through ideological consciousness. Technical training of the work force is needed and qualitative and quantitative increases of the means of production.

In other words, changes in levels of productive forces development will be achieved through *accumulation as a process utilizing the economic surplus of society*. In under-developed societies, this surplus comes mainly from the agricultural sector as from primary production in general. This surplus should therefore be studied: its volume, the activities that generate it, the type of production units out of which it comes, the forms of money revenues in which it manifests itself, etc.

Economic surplus: why do we stress this surplus? Because it represents the point of departure to unmask the principal false concept which plagues us: the presumed lack of capital in an under-developed society. The Egyptian peasant has always produced a considerable surplus. He has done so since the second agricultural revolution which took place just before the beginning of written history, and which led to the appearance of cities in the Nile Valley, over 50 centuries ago. The use of this surplus took various forms: in addition to feeding the city, it was used to build pyramids, temples, churches and mosques. Throughout history, the peasants saw their surplus mobilized by the city, up to the arrival of Bonaparte at the end of the 18th century. Bonaparte arrived from Paris bringing not only the veterans of previous campaigns (the so-called "grognards") but also capitalist rationality. This was the first direct confrontation between Egyptian society and this morbid rationality. A team of scientists surveyed Egypt and, for the first time, the whole of Egyptian society was considered as one huge enterprise: what were its resources? how were they to be used? what surplus could be reaped from it? After the attempt of Mohamed Ali (1805-1840) to build a sort of centralized capitalist economy, the aggressivity of capital managed to integrate the Egyptian economy into the world capitalist economy. And the Egyptian peasant continued to produce a surplus, but in new ways, i.e. corresponding to the needs of the metropolitan economy. During World War I and World War II, Egyptian society was forced to save 22 to 25% of its national income to finance the war effort. This saving was accumulated in what was called the "sterling balance". To finance war efforts, a surplus could be found. Is it not strange that to finance economic and social development, that same surplus does not seem to exist anymore? That is all history to be sure, but it is crucial if we want to know ourselves, to understand the present and to evaluate our potential future development, although we are often invited to forget it or to misread this history.

Once the surplus is located, the next problem is *to mobilize* it in order to develop productive forces. This implies an evaluation of the various mobilization techniques: taxes, prices, reorganization of production units and commercial institutions, etc.

The path of development by structural changes needed to achieve the primary goal (the newly-defined consumption pattern) will be determined by the volume of accumulation, i.e. by the amount of invested surplus, and by the pattern of accumulation, i.e. the way investment resources are allocated between agriculture, industry, and services, as well as by the type of agricultural and industrial projects chosen.

As to the *volume of accumulation*, it is not necessary to sacrifice the present by limiting sharply current consumption in order to increase investment. However, all superfluous consumption must be eliminated. Furthermore, one should always bear in mind that the productivity of direct producers is determined by their level of consumption as well as by the form of organization, political mobilization, the dominant value-system, etc. It is also necessary to increase by a comparatively larger proportion the consumption levels of the lower classes among the population. This increase has to parallel investment growth. Consumption and investment will increase, *in absolute terms*, with, possibly, a comparatively greater rate of increase in investment.

As to the mode of accumulation, it is determined by the respective shares of agriculture, industry, and services in the accumulated means of production, the type of activity to foster in each sector, and the geographic location of new projects in each of the three fields.

The allocation of resources between the various sectors of use can be computed (centrally), by economic calculation, on the basis of prices (the law of value), a means linked to a merchant economy, by political decision, or by a combination of both. In which case either prices would be subordinated to politics or market-prices would predominate.

Which pattern should be adopted? It depends on the type of inter-class alliance (of peasants and workers, affecting the relation of agriculture and industry.) Thus it depends on the socio-political nature of the State, on the State's capacity to maintain this alliance, which in itself requires a certain balance between the sectors of activity (the nature of this balance and its achievement depending on the actual conditions under which the strategy for social and economic development operates.) We come back to the essential problem: that of the State in our society, its socio-political nature, its class structure: is it a State of direct producers or a State of other classes or social strata, mainly the middle classes and petite bourgeoisie?

One could determine the modalities for accumulation in light of the following considerations.

In *agriculture*, the long-term goal would be to transform it into an industrial sector, in which science and technology could be applied. *What kind of agriculture should be stressed?* That will depend on the type of existing production. If it is specializing in food products, one should in part and over time, transform it into an agriculture producing food appropriate for the masses (sufficiently diversified in terms of nutritive value.) If, in addition to food production, there is primary production (mining, petroleum), both agriculture and industry could be transformed while consumption could simultaneously greatly increase, there is also the problem of transforming rural society, that might reduce the contradiction between town and country. This might be achieved, in a first phase, by rural industrialization, permitting local production, be it at a very modest scale, of consumption and production goods necessary for the rural community. In a second phase, one could envisage de-urbanization of the large cities, over-population is the process of creating under-development.

In *industry* and in related mining sectors, the long-term objective ought to be the setting-up of basic industries and those enterprises necessary for the manufacturing of production goods as defined by the consumption pattern.

Which element in industry would be stressed? This depends on tive ought to be the setting-up of basic industries and those enter-on the need to create an industrial base such that the necessary industrial conditions for the development of agriculture could be achieved, and independence is guaranteed.

As far as *the technical form of projects* is concerned, there should be a blend of carefully-chosen foreign techniques and internally-developed ones. Here we have to count on the innovative capacity of producers. In fact, the final result would be a combination of techniques in projects of each sector, with varying ratios of labor and productive factors. One should recall that for some types of projects, the choice is limited, and that, in general, all other things being equal, the higher the quality and quantity of factors of production, the higher will be labour productivity.

These techniques are never neutral. For example, given a quantity of resources for the building of dams, the choice will be either to build a limited number of large dams (with all that this implies in technical terms) or to build a large number of small dams scattered throughout vast areas. In the first case, a large dam enables one to irrigate a large area mainly to provide for city markets inside and outside the country. Numerous small dams may better satisfy the needs of small direct producers by favouring immediate consumption of the production. Another example: in order to increase food production, e.g. wheat, the expansion can be of soft wheat or of hard wheat. Soft wheat is mainly consumed in the cities while hard wheat is for hard-working people: peasants and labourers.

As for *services*, the whole concept should be re-thought. For example:

Education: Given the particular cultural background, a new educational pattern must be developed, and to do this, people should not forget that education and real life struggle are but a single process. We should not forget either that the main purpose of education will be to remodel "mentalities" by establishing a value-system which refutes the concepts previously established and upheld by capitalist society. The objective would be a type of man who, while specialized, could at one and the same time engage in productive work, be active in political life, and so on. To do this, we shall have to link productive labor to the process of learning. This implies a new meaning to the right to education. Not only will people have the right to *obtain* an education, as in capitalist societies, but also the right to *practice* it. Educational reform must have as its goal the transformation of men from passive recipients to active participants and, finally, to prime "actors". When man is respected as such and when the exercise of his sovereign rights is guaranteed, he acts without having to rely on material reward. This would create a new perspective on stimulating production and continuous political struggle.

Health: Given the limited resources available during the initial phase, special attention must be paid to preventive medicine to fight chronic diseases. At the same time, small clinical units should be created. Personnel need not have advanced training, but would necessarily live among direct producers.

Housing: In the initial phase, decent housing should be provided to lower classes of the population. Later on, a new concept of housing should be devised: They should not necessarily be large, but should be built at the loci of production; they should be built by the producers themselves, using techniques they can master, and local building materials

With respect to the *location of new production activities*, it might be decided according to the following criteria: Resources available in the area; the obligation to respect the cultural heritage; the necessity for each area to produce a minimum variety of products; the services provided should be accessible to the direct producers.

With respect to the *location of industrial projects*, one should distinguish: Industrial projects which are essential to the nation as a whole; industrial projects which are essential for regions; and industrial projects which ought to be located as close as possible to the consumers. Placing industries should, during the initial phase, specifically take into consideration the needs of the country, mainly the lower classes of rural population, and of the lower classes in the urban population.

The development process should not take the form of the expansion of urbanization as discussed in the context of current regional analysis, but rather a process of industrialization of the countryside, eventually accompanied at a later stage by de-urbanization. This is the possible framework for an Alternative Development Strategy. The fundamental idea in this regard is the elaboration of a strategy according to social criteria and not profit-making criteria. In other words, it is conceived from a value perspective totally different from that type of social organization which created underdevelopment.

This alternative strategy raises some transitional problems among which the most important are the problem related to society's reorganization in the political sphere, i.e. the constitution of a new type of State, and the problem related to foreign trade, for the plan's objectives require imports. An under-developed economy has at present no choice. Present conditions of the world market are to be taken as given. Within this framework, imports should be kept at a minimum and in the short run, *gains in foreign exchange* should be maximized by improving the terms of trade (either through prices or through the geographical redistribution of foreign trade), in order to cover the costs of imports. Imports should be selective and stress machinery. Moreover, even if there is a balance between resources and internal needs, there could still be an imbalance in the need for imported goods and the gains from export. If we want to do without foreign capital, we may substitute foreign credit, provided it does not alter the conditions necessary to pursue our strategy.

It is quite clear that the achievement of this type of alternative development strategy requires a new socio-political framework based on the free mobilization of the mass of direct producers. Its achievement should be the first priority. What shall we do in the meantime? First of all, we should participate in political action aimed at putting into effect this alternative strategy. Then we must, individually or in groups, pursue research on the various aspects of this strategy. Finally, each time we have the opportunity to advise on a course of action or to participate in some action, our advice or participation should lean in the direction of this alternative development strategy.

Whatever the immediate role that each one of us can play, no effort should be spared to speed up the process of transformation, whatever its nature, taking place in our societies. Indeed, the faster the process, the sooner will come the time when the limits of the present forms of organization will become apparent, as will their incapacity to solve the fundamental problems of under-development in our societies.

NOTES

(1) The argument presented here is based on a knowledge of the situation in various African countries, and especially Egypt and Algeria.
(2) By direct producers we mean those who participate (or will participate) effectively (or eventually) in the social process of work by utilizing factors of production, whether or not they are presently so involved, for one reason or another.
(3) For the Latin-American cases, see M. Ikonicoff, « Les deux étapes de la croissance en Amérique latine », document presented at the IDEP seminar on Development Strategies Applicable to African Landlocked Countries, Bamako, March 1973.
(4) To talk about capital on the international market does not mean there exists only "national" capital or only "international" capital. At the international level, there are in fact several national capitals which compete for the world market. While the strategies of various national capitals differ one can distinguish, at a certain stage of the system's development as a whole, some general strategy of capital.
(5) We say transition *in the direction of* (pour) and not *towards* (vers), because we don't wish to convey the impression that this transition is guaranteed once all these conditions are satisfied or that it will happen without risk or regression. This transformation is a dialectical process, achieved through solving the contradictions. It thus involves a struggle, a long struggle in which set-backs are possible. Reconstruction goes on with its continuities and its discontinuities. This is why we prefer to talk about transition *in the direction of* a socialist society.
(6) In terms of the situation of the international capitalist economy in general, the specificity of the present stage must be found in the specific form of relationships of capital and labour within this economy. To arrive at this specific form one should study international capital (the unity of international capital, national or international companies; the composition of international capital and its contradictions, American capital, Japanese capital, European capital, etc.; the phenomenon of hegemony; the functioning of capital in developed parts of the capitalist world; bloc formation and movements of capital between advanced capitalist countries; the relationship of labour and capital and movements of wages, profits and prices over time; changes in the production systems and the forms of international capitalist division of labour, etc.)
(7) Even for the present capitalist society, it appears from recent research that material stimuli are no longer as effective as before. After all, why should we work more if the working conditions are those of alienation under its various forms? People now are beginning to seek new *raisons d'être*.

ECONOMIC DEVELOPMENT IN CANADA

Mel Watkins

The approach here draws specifically on a Canadian approach to economic history, but that approach has, since World War II, been so eroded by Americanization that we now have much more to learn from the concepts developed by Latin American scholars than Latin Americans have from us. It is true that reference is sometimes made, in Latin American and elsewhere, to the "Canadian model of development", that is, industrialization through import-substitution under the aegis of foreign-based multinational corporations. There is, in fact, an important sense in which Canada pioneered an industrial strategy, the limitations of which have been increasingly experienced by other countries which have followed it. Nevertheless, a longer view requires us to see that Canada, relative to Latin America, is a special case which has permitted it to become so dependent and yet so rich.

Prof. Watkins would liked it to be noted that this paper was presented in April, 1975 and that since then R.T. Naylor's "The History of Canadian Business", and LAWG's "Falconbridge" have been published.

The Canadian experience, culminating in its present truncated industrial structure, must be looked at in the context of Canada's history as a staple exporting country. We can then see how Canada's export-orientation from the outset has created a class structure that has not only distorted but suppressed industrial development. The role of the multinational corporation since the latter part of the last century has been critical to keeping Canada locked into that pattern.[1] It follows that the multinational corporation, being part of the problem, is unlikely to be part of the solution.

From a global perspective, the essential characteristics of Canada as a capitalist country are that it is rich and dependent. In the words of Professor James Laxer of York University:

> "a central contemporary dilemma conditions the questions Canadians want answered when they study their history. How can Canada be so rich and at the same time so dependent on an outside country — the United States? Or to ask the obverse question: if Canada is so dependent on the United States, why is it so well off compared to other countries in the American empire?"[2]

The answer is to be found by going back to Canada's colonial origins. As European man spread globally, the motive was trade and the establishing of colonies which would produce staples for export to Europe in return for European manufactured goods. In a limited number of cases, what was found were vast empty lands — or, more accurately, areas sparsely populated with aboriginal peoples who were decimated or pushed aside. The description fits not only Canada but also the United States, Australia, New Zealand and in a limited sense South Africa, that is, the United States and the white Dominions or, following the League of Nations, areas of recent settlement. Canadian historians, notably H.A. Innis, developed what can be called a staple theory of economic growth to describe the Canadian case; it would have application to other "new countries", but is necessarily not a general theory of growth or even of colonial growth.[3]

Two Canadian economic historians have recently shed some light on the question posed by Laxer. Professor John Hutcheson of York University observes:[4]

> "There are... a few areas of the world where European expansion has resulted in the development of prosperous capitalist economies. One area is North America. For the U.S. the only obstacle to accumulation and capitalist expansion was foreign domination. The bourgeoisie in that

country was strong enough to overthrow that domination and to create a
political framework conducive to the growth of capitalism" (p. 165)

He argues, following Andre Gunder Frank, that from the outset
colonial societies, including Canada, were tied to the capitalist world
market, but he agrees with Frank's critics that it does not follow that
the colonies developed capitalist relations of production from the
beginning, which, following Marx, requires a free labourer selling his
labour-power, that is, a capitalist labour market.

He proceeds:

"in a comparative analysis of dependent societies it is of particular importance to investigate the extent to which capitalist integration has been
achieved.... The degree of capitalist integration is undoubtedly *one* factor in the prosperity of the dependent society.... In Canada an almost
fully-integrated capitalist social structure *did* grow out of a colonial society which was already integrated into a capitalist empire. Though the
key factor in Canada's development has been the extraction of a series
of staple products by a series of imperial powers, Canada has never
been *merely* a resource colony. Canada is unlike other colonies in which
capitalism promoted plantation production, using slavery or indentured
labour, or perpetuated various forms of non-capitalist production based
on peasant labour. Canada has become a fully integrated capitalist society, that is a society with capitalist property relations, and a society in
which the overwhelming proportion of the population is engaged in
capitalist production. It is perhaps for this reason that Canada, despite
its colonial aspects, has developed into a rich country." (p. 166)

Professor R. T. Naylor of McGill University, in a far-reaching
reexamination of Canadian economic history, lays bare the
mechanism by which Canada could emerge as a capitalist and yet
dependent economy. Drawing on the staples approach and the Canadian experience, he writes:

"The dominance of a few staples leads not to independent capitalist development but to the perpetuation of colonialism and underdevelopment.[5]

"Colonial economies produce staple goods — fish, furs, wheat, wood and
minerals, for export to the imperium and import finished products; and
the group who control the export and import, and the relations with the
imperium are a mercantile capitalist class."[6]

This class, whose bias is to operate in the sphere of circula-
tion, is to be contrasted with the industrial capitalist class, which
necessarily operates centrally in the sphere of production. For
Naylor, "The greatest contradiction among the strata of the
bourgeoisie appears between the industrial-capitalist entrepreneur

and the mercantile-financial entrepreneur."[7] Canadian history becomes the story of how the mercantile class has maintained dominance as *the* indigenous capitalist class. Industrialization has taken place, not under the control of Canadian capitalists, but rather predominantly, and increasingly over time, of foreign-based, mostly American, multinational corporations. The indigenous Canadian industrial capitalist class is hence mostly a comprador class, subservient on the one hand to the greater power of the Canadian mercantile-financial class, and yet more subservient to the power of the American industrial capitalists, who control the branch plants which they merely manage. The sum of all this is that the Canadian mercantile-financial capitalist class, in the very process of suppressing an *indigenous* industrial capitalist class necessarily renders itself, and hence the Canadian state which it originally created in its own image, subservient to the American corporations and their American state.

Contemporary data on foreign ownership in Canada is fully consistent with this historical analysis. As Wallace Clement of Carleton University puts it:

> "The strength of Canadian capitalists, today and historically, lies in the finance, transportation and utilities sectors of the economy ... Foreign control is greatest in the surplus creating sectors of manufacturing and resources but Canadian control is dominant in the 'service' sectors and areas of circulation..."[8]

Naylor's analysis is not only a logical extension of the staple theory and of Canadian historiography. It also has powerful roots in the Marxist tradition. For Marx himself, the development of industry, or industrial capital, required merchant capital to be relegated to a secondary position. There is an evolutionary link between merchant capital and finance capital — and this is evident in the Canadian case in the movement from mercantile-based fishing and fur-trading activities to banks, insurance companies and investment houses, and from short-term merchant capital to the long-term finance capital undertaken by Canadian mercantile elites in the canal and railway booms — but the full development of industrial capital requires overthrowing the dominance of mercantile-finance capital.[9] Paul Baran,[10] in considering the impact of the imperium on its colonies, argued that imperialism has worked to strengthen mercantile capitalism in the underdeveloped countries; Naylor shows how British finance imperialism and American corporate imperialism have done exactly that in the Canadian case. Frank suggests that "the global extension and unity of the capitalist system, its monopoly structure and uneven development throughout its history" has resulted in the "persistence of commercial rather than industrial capitalism in the underdeveloped world (including its most industrially advanced countries).[11]

For almost a century we have lived in the era of the multinational corporation and of direct investment. Following Naylor: "Empires built on direct investment are the highest stage of imperialism... Direct investment empires are founded on the take-over of the actual production process, and they grow on their own volition by reinvestment of alienated hinterland surplus."[12] Corporate imperialism created comprador industrial bourgeoisies in the hinterlands: "While multinational corporations do not, as so often claimed, internationalize their managements, they do denationalize a section of the native bourgeoisies in the countries they penetrate. This of course weakens native bourgeoisies..."[13]

Now of the "new countries", their affluence notwithstanding, only the United States has broken out of the pattern of dependent capitalism; predictably, it has become a leading example of capitalist imperialism. While not central to this paper to explain why in any detail, we can agree with Hutcheson — and with Paul Baran, William Appleman Williams and others — that the only obstacle to independent capitalism was foreign domination; the obverse of this, of course, is that the failure to remove that obstacle, as in Canada is sufficient to explain — indeed, it defines — the persistence of dependency. The very ability of the United States to free itself meant it had the capacity to impose its domain over the Americas, including Canada, and hence reduced their prospects for independence.

The burden of the argument to this point is that Canada is not Latin America or the Caribbean because of fuller capitalist integration from an early point, and hence it is richer, but neither is it the United States — or Germany and Japan — because a full-blown industrial capitalist class does not emerge, and hence it is dependent.

We are now in a position to look more specifically at Canadian industrialization. Its serious development dates from the 1850's, though breweries (Molson) and flourmills (Ogilvie) flowed from the surplus — which mostly, however, remained as mercantile-financial capital — created by the fur trade and by currency manipulation after the conquest of New France,[14] and first lumber and then paper companies (Price, now merged with Abitibi) flowed from the surpluses that accrued to what were originally the Canadian branches of the great British timber houses engaged in the trade in square timber.

An important route by which more advanced American technique entered Canada in the early period was via the migration of American entrepreneurs. (For example, Hiram Walker moved from Massachusetts in 1857 and established his distillery.) In the nature of the case, those who succeeded became indigenous Canadian capitalists, and fortunes were founded that in some cases survive as independent Canadian companies down to the present day. This is in sharp contrast to the later period, post-approximately-1880, when the northward migration of American technique increasingly took the form of branch plants which did not tend to evolve into independent Canadian companies. Also, industries or firms established in the boom of the 1850's were more likely to survive as Canadian entities than those founded later because they got a head start on the U.S. multinationals; an important case in point are the farm implement manufacturers, Massey and Harris, which are the precursors of one of the very few present-day Canadian-based industrial multinationals, Massey Ferguson.

But we must not exaggerate the strength of early, pre-American-invasion, industrialization. The abortive rebellions of the 1830's in what are now Ontario and Quebec left the commercial class firmly in control — to the extent that control resided in British North America — which is in sharp contrast with the rise of the industrial class to dominance in both Great Britain and the U.S. in this period. That commercial class, closely allied with British financiers, was able to solidify its position by creating its version of the state with Confederation in 1867.

Within a little more than a decade, Canada moved to a high protective tariff which, probably by design, was a policy not of creating infant Canadian firms but rather industrialization by invitation — to American companies to establish branch plants. The tariff itself was only one part of a broader National Policy including railway subsidies — and a consequent inflow of British portfolio capital as infrastructure for the branch plants; an open door to immigration — and hence a pool of labour and an expanding domestic market for the branch plants; a patent system which, like the tariff, compelled

American companies previously exporting to Canada to manufacture in Canada; subsidies to foreign corporations via competitive bonussing by municipalities;[15] and provincial give-aways of rights to lumber and to mine Crown land, where Americans with prior experience in raping and looting at home tended to have an advantage.[16]

The effect of all this was an inward rush of branch plants. By World War I, while the ratio of foreign, particularly American, ownership was significantly lower than it was to become, particularly after World War II, there is clear evidence of the dominance of U.S. capital in key industrial sectors. In 1914, U.S. branch plants accounted for about 10 percent of total capital invested in Canadian industry, but Glen Williams has recently pointed out[17] that U.S. branch plants tended to dominate by ownership and/or licensing arrangements the electrical industries, the chemical industries, and industries based on application of the internal combustion engine, and that these industries are, following Eric Hobsbawn (and others) the three major growth industries of the Second Industrial Revolution.

In spite of the clearly neo-colonial character of Canadian policy, in the period down to World War I and into the interwar period the Canadian economy functioned remarkably well. The key reason for this was expansion into resource-rich internal frontiers, specifically, the opening for settlement and for wheat production for export to Europe of the Canadian West, and the exploitation, which became increasingly intense after World War I, of the forests and minerals of the Canadian Shield for export to the U.S. While this is well-known and its importance may seem obvious, its significance for Canadian prosperity and for the nature of Canadian capitalism deserves to be thought through. As Frank has observed from his studies of Brazil and Chile,[18] outside metropolitan domination does not preclude, but virtually necessitates, a colonial sub-metropolis which then administers and exploits, albeit for a higher purpose, internal hinterlands; if the sub-metropolis is sufficiently fortunate in its hinterlands it could move, at least in part, by their exploitation to its own independence, that is, become a metropolis in its own right. Given the richness of Canada's resources, one might have expected some significant movement along these lines. The failure of anything like this to happen must be put down to the entrenched position of the commercial class leading to the veritable flood of branch plants from the U.S., which assured that the internal empire would be based on control of trade rather than control of industrialization proper. British financial capital and U.S. corporate capital created jobs and a rising standard of living — which removed much of the possibility of mass discontent with the strategy of dependence — while the Canadian mercantile class, as intermediaries, got what it wanted by skimming off surplus. As Naylor puts it: "Canada would not be a colony were colonial status not of material benefit both to the metropolis whose colony it is and to the indigenous ruling class";[19] we need only add that, in the final analysis, there must also be sufficient general prosperity to pacify the working class, unless there is a willingness to resort to serious and persistent repression.

The extent of industrialization, in quantitative terms, is a tribute as well to what has been called the sub-imperial strategy.[20] The Canadian ruling class saw Canada as that part of the British Empire where U.S. companies manufactured for imperial markets, that is, Australia, New Zealand, South Africa, the British Caribbean, India, British Malaya, but typically not Britain itself. Both the American and British ruling classes, still more or less equally poised, found such an arrangement sensible and profitable under the circumstances, while the ruling classes of the British dependencies were in no position to take serious objection. Canada sometimes got an additional benefit by having the Latin American market tossed in as well for its American subsidiaries so as to permit greater economies of scale. So it was that by the late 1920's Canada was the third largest auto producer in the world, second only to the U.S. and Great Britain, and exporting more than half its output in spite of being almost wholly American-owned.

In the nature of things, that is, of capitalism where there is always someone lower down, Canada was also a mini-imperialist in the area of direct investment. Much has been made on occasion of the fact that Canadians are bigger investors abroad on a per capital basis than Americans. Even cursory knowledge of the facts shows that this Canadian "imperialism" hardly deserves to be called even mini-imperialism; rather, it fits into a sub-imperial pattern that is, if anything, even more subordinate than the trade pattern. Canadian *direct* investment abroad, which is considerably less than total investment, is mostly, as one would expect, in the sectors where Canadian capitalists are strong, namely, railways, banks and utilities, and mostly in the U.S.; direct investment by a small country in a large country clearly has different effects than the reverse. Canadian direct investment other than in the United States was often by the Canadian subsidiaries of U.S. corporations; for example, Ford of Canada had subsidiaries in a number of British dependencies. We can agree with Naylor[21] that: "Canada's parasitical pseudo-imperialist ventures conform precisely to the pattern of development of Canadian capitalism itself."[22]

For almost a century — from the Reciprocity Treaty with the U.S. and the beginning of an active staple trade in a north-south direction around the middle of the 19th century to the final collapse of the formal British Empire around the middle of the 20th — Canadian capitalism was dependent on two metropoles, the U.S. and the U.K. Compared to the earlier and the later period, Canada had a bit more room to manoeuvre, and there was at times at least the illusion of independence. But whatever opportunity there may have been to create an indigenous industrial capitalist class was scrupulously avoided.

An aspect that has been insufficiently emphasized, though clearly inherent in Naylor's analysis, is the role of foreign capital itself in suppressing domestic capital. The mechanisms of the suppression need greater specification. At the macro-level, surplus generated under foreign control is either reinvested or paid out to shareholders (typically, the foreign parent). In the former case, foreign ownership is directly perpetuated; in the latter, the initial inflow of capital sets up a perpetual outflow which inhibits the formation of capital within the surplus-producing country. Eric Kierans of McGill University, who is as well a former Canadian Cabinet Minister and now an advisor to provincial governments on resource policy, describes the process on the resource side:[23]

> "Resource rich nations that continually yield up the value of their wealth in return for the labour employed in its exploitation will never be more than resource nations. They lose the opportunity to form their own capital, capital which will enable them to break out of that very reliance on their resource base and reduce their dependence on foreign investment."

Kierans has documented the extent of the outward drain of surplus in metal mining in Manitoba. On the manufacturing side, a dramatic example is provided by Ford. Ford Motor Company of Canada Ltd. was founded in 1904 by a Canadian with an initial capitalization of $125,000. Fifty-one percent was given to the Ford

Motor Company of Detroit in return for all Ford rights and processes in Canada, New Zealand, Australia, India, Union of South Africa and British Malaya. On the initial capitalization of $125,000,
only part of which was paid in cash, the company paid cash dividends of close to $15 million between 1905 and 1927, and the in-
crease of almost $7 million in issued capital during those years was
entirely by way of stock dividends. [24]

A major gap in Canadian economic history is detailed study, on
an industry-by-industry basis, of the interrelationship of foreign and
domestic capital. Naylor's approach is through the financial institutions, that is, demonstrating how their behaviour disadvantaged
Canadian industrialists; there is need for complementary micro-level
research within the productive sphere itself. [25] A hypothesis that
merits testing is that a critical mechanism by which foreign capital
suppresses domestic capital is by the former's influence over the
Canadian state, that is, that American capital has used the Canadian
state directly, and indirectly through the U.S. state, to suppress
Canadian capital.

A case in point, is nickel, an industry whose history is well
documented. [26] Though the massive ore body at Sudbury was discovered while building the Canadian Pacific Railway and was initially
the property of Canadian speculators, it quickly fell into the hands
of Americans who had not only the capital, but also the essential contacts with the U.S. Navy. Support from the latter facilitated the development of the refining technology in the hands of the Orford Copper
Co. in New Jersey, and the refinery was then located there; power
gravitated toward it and away from the Canadian Copper Company
which merely owned the ore and was, in any event, American-dominated. Agitation for refining in Canada faced the powerful obstacle,
after 1890, that nickel ore and matte, but not refined nickel, were
on the U.S. free list.

Samuel Ritchie, the founder of Canadian Copper, an American
resident for some time in Canada, and an advocate of a Canadian
refinery was pushed out of the company by his Ohio financial back-
ers in the 1890's, whereupon he allied himself with an established
group of industrialists from Hamilton, Ontario who not only possessed the financial and technical resources to build a nickel-steel complex but were substantial supporters of the new Laurier Liberal
Government. Robert M. Thompson of Orford was able, by threats of
turning to New Caledonia — from where the French Rothschild's Le

Nickel drew its ore — to get Laurier to resist the pressure. Stymied at the federal level, the Ritchie-Hamilton group persuaded the new Ross Liberal Government in Ontario to amend the Mining Act such as virtually to compel nickel refining in Ontario, but Thompson was able to get Laurier to threaten disallowance of this legislation and the Provincial Government weakened and never proclaimed the bill. Consistent with the Naylor thesis, the general manager of Canada's largest bank weighed in on the side of Thompson against economic nationalism.

As evidence of Canadian benefit, Thompson at one point informed Laurier that his company was paying out as much in wages to Canadians as it was dividends to the American owners. Shortly thereafter the director of the Ontario Bureau of Mines calculated that more than two-thirds of the value of the ores mined at Sudbury was distributed in wages and expenses at refineries in the U.S., and this did not include processing to armour plate.

The monopoly power of Orford was solidified when the leading manufacturer of nickel-steel armour plate, United States Steel, and its banker, the House of Morgan, merged Canadian Copper and Orford into the International Nickel Co. Agitation for home manufacture continued in Canada. Inco continued to use successfully the threat of New Caledonia ores, though it was clearly a ruse by 1905 when Canada permanently overtook New Caledonia as the world's most important source of nickel. There were allegations that J.P. Morgan & Co. through their control in the New York capital market played an important role in bankrupting one potential competitor — Francis Clergue's combined nickel and steel operations — and in the case of the Ritchie-Hamilton group we are told that Morgan successfully prevented the leading American smelter companies from purchasing the company's property after the group had lost the political wars.

The final evidence for the view that the Canadian state was used by foreign capital, in this case Inco, is provided by Nelles. In 1906 "Thompson sent Laurier a cheque for an undisclosed amount which included a 'profit of $5,000 on stock which Thompson claimed to have purchased for the Prime Minister''; Laurier made an "effusive reply".

Inco finally shifted its refinery to Ontario only after the great scandal that blew up around its selling nickel to Germany during World War I — when Canada was at war with Germany but the

U.S. had not yet entered — which led to public agitation demanding public ownership. Incidentally, the British Admiralty was convinced that German U-boats did load nickel refined in the U.S. from Canadian ore, but Prime Minister Borden refused to believe it. At the same time, the most serious potential competitor to be faced by Inco, the British American Nickel Corporation, emerged — backed by F.S. Pearson, a New York entrepreneur who had led Canadian capital into steel, street railways and South American utilities; E.R. Wood, President of Dominion Securities and founder of Brazilian Traction, precursor of Brascan; and James Dunn who went on to create Algoma Steel, now part of Canadian Pacific Investments, from the ashes of the Clergue empire. Inco's timely move froze them out and Inco picked up their refining technology, which was superior to its own and was to be the basis of another great round of Inco prosperity. Having eliminated both of the viable alternatives, public ownership and British American, Inco merged with Ludwig Mond of Wales in the 1920's to make its monopoly of Canadian ores complete. At the same time, Falconbridge emerged as a competitor based on Canadian ores, but it was not to become a substantial company until after World War II, at which time it fell under American control.

The key struggle exemplified by this case is the suppression of domestic capital by foreign capital, both through Inco's monopoly power in product and capital markets and, above all, by its power to influence the Canadian state consistently to favour foreign capital over both private Canadian capital and public ownership.

Closely intertwined therewith is the story of how forward linkage into further processing was blocked by foreign capital. A recent study by Pierre L. Bourgault for the Science Council of Canada notes:

"We are the world's largest producer of nickel, but we are net importers of stainless steel and manufactured nickel products...; we are the world's second largest producer of aluminum, but we import it in its most sophisticated forms such as... precision aluminum parts for use in aircraft; we are the world's largest exporter of pulp and paper, but we import much of our fine paper and virtually all of the highly sophisticated paper, such as backing for photographic film; we are one of the world's principal sources of platinum, but it is all exported for refining and processing and reimported in finished forms; we are large exporters of natural gas and petroleum, but we are net importers of petrochemicals; and although we are the world's foremost exporter of raw asbestos fibres, we are net importers of manufactured asbestos products." [27]

This is striking evidence of the pervasiveness of the problem, and given what we know about the extent and nature of foreign ownership in both the resource and manufacturing sectors, is highly suggestive, to say the least, of the ability of foreign capital to distort and suppress industrial development.

Writing in the mid-1930's, the authors of the only serious attempt at detailed historical analysis of foreign ownership in Canada [28] argued that the Canadian economy was maturing and the need for foreign capital in the future would lessen. They could not have been more wrong — and given their eminence as economists there is surely a moral here. The decade after World War II saw a quantum leap in American direct investment in Canada. Between 1945 and 1957, U.S. direct investment in Canada increased in total from $2.3 billion to $8.5 billion; in manufacturing from $1.3 billion to $3.6 billion, and in mining and smelting — a key staple sector — from $250 million to $3.3 billion. Between 1946 and 1957 foreign, mostly American, control of manufacturing increased from 35 per cent to 56 per cent, and in mining and smelting from 38 per cent to 70 per cent. Rising U.S. investment in Canada, in turn, facilitated a dramatic switch in the immediate postwar years in the direction of Canadian trade. The traditional pattern had been that 65 per cent of exports went overseas and 35 per cent to the U.S. By 1950 these figures had exactly reversed themselves, while the predominant role of the U.S. as supplier of imports remained unchanged.

These massive changes in investment and trade were central to a process by which Canada finally abandoned a sinking British Empire and entered fully into the American Empire. The Canadian philosopher, George Grant, has written: [29]

"From 1940 to 1957, the ruling class of this country was radically reshaped. In 1939, the United Kingdom still seemed a powerful force, and the men who ruled Canada were a part of the old Atlantic triangle. They turned almost as much to Great Britain as to the United States, economically, culturally and politically. After 1940, the ruling class found its centre of gravity in the United States."

Canada's preeminent Tory historian, Donald Creighton, summarizes the totality of the experience: [30]

"Since 1940, Canada has been exposed to the irresistable penetrative power of American economic and military imperialism. The process by which the Dominion became a branch plant dependency and a military satellite of the American Republic began with the Ogdensburg Agreement of 1940 (which committed Canada to a permanent military alliance with the U.S.); and since then Canada's subordination of American foreign policy and American capital has continued progressively with scarcely a serious interruption. Canada joined NATO largely because the United States was certain to do so. Canada was taken in by the confidence trick which President Truman and his aides practised on the United Nations in 1950 and, like Britain, agreed to accept American leadership in the Korean War. Canada consented to the American fortification of her northland, and thus implicitly permitted her defence policy to be determined by the anti-Communist mania which swept over the United States in the 1950's. In the meantime, under the benevolent supervision of C.D. Howe (a senior Cabinet Minister), the economic continentalist who was (Prime Minister) King's perfect associate, American ownership of industry grew apace.''

With the end of World War II, the elaborate machinery that tied the Canadian military system into the American military system was not dismantled. At the same time, the U.S. moved quickly to the invention of the Cold War, thereby avoiding any risk of a return to the 1930's and assuring, by military means, a world safe for its multinational corporations.

In Canada too the immediate necessity after World War II was to maintain economic prosperity and avoid another Great Depression that would trigger off labour militancy and create fertile ground for anti-capitalist politics. The key as to how this was done is to be found in the relationship between the Canadian state and foreign capital.

In April 1945, as the war was drawing to a close in Europe, the Government pledged in a White Paper on Employment and Income to maintain a high level of employment and growth. Though influenced in its rhetoric by the Keynesian theory of fiscal policy, that is, public spending and the maintenance of purchasing power through lower taxes and a more developed welfare state, the essential reality was to be the reinforcement of traditional strategies of capitalist growth appropriate to a dependent economy. In effect, the Government's actual growth strategy was the subsidizing of private capital formation without respect to the nationality of capital, which in practice favoured larger-scale foreign capital over domestic capital.

Millions of dollars worth of war plants had been constructed and operated by the Government during the war. Under Howe, as

Minister of Reconstruction, these plants were sold and leased to private industry, generally at one-third or less of their original construction cost. [31]

David Wolfe has looked in some detail at the incentive effects for foreign capital of Canada's postwar fiscal policy. [32] During the war, Howe had engineered the development of a new fiscal tool, the fast tax write-off through accelerated depreciation rates. In November 1944 the technique was incorporated into law until March 1949 to cover reconversion, and provided "one of the fastest rates of tax write-offs in the western world". Accompanied by a host of other incentives, for example, immediate write-offs of expenditures for R&D and concessions to encourage exploration and drilling for minerals and oil, the result was "the most comprehensive industrial development program employed in this country to that time." In 1949, the new Income Tax Act built in higher depreciation rates in the initial years of the use of the asset as a permanent feature. A later Royal Commission study [33] was to conclude that this feature of the tax act, much more generous than in either the U.S. or the U.K., was probably the strongest inducement to foreign investment in Canada. As well, during the Korean War, Howe was again given extraordinary powers with respect to accelerated depreciation rates, and he used them to promote the Alcan plant at Kitimat, B.C. (which was written off before it began operations), the expansion of Canadair, and the initial undertaking of the Iron Ore Co. of Canada's operations in the Ungava peninsula.

What is evident is not merely the open door to foreign capital, but the greasing of the skids with Canadian tax dollars. [34] As we have seen, the foreign capital did indeed flood in. The Canadian Government was delighted. In a speech in October 1949, Howe told his audience with pride that U.S. investments in Canada were "paying a bigger cash return to American investors than all other American investments abroad put together." "Some 2,000 American companies and branches are now established in this country", he said, and "We hope that more American companies will avail themselves of the favourable conditions for investment in Canada".

The dramatic changes in trade and investment did not take place without some friction, and the manner in which that was dealt with is also instructive. Difficulties in selling to Britain, in spite of large-scale loans by Canada, at a time when imports from the U.S. were rising, created a severe dollar crisis for Canada by late 1947.

Abbott, the Minister of Finance, set up controls and restrictions on imports, the effect of which was to increase for the long-term the number of American industrial branch plants in Canada. At the same time, Abbott stated that Canada would seek to develop natural resources for export to the U.S. so as to reduce permanently the lack of balance in Canadian — American trade — the so-called Abbott Plan. In April 1948 the proclamation of the Marshall Plan by the U.S. completed the process of pulling Canada out of the impasse. The U.S. permitted recipients to make Marshall Plan purchases in Canada, and in the following year $700 million of Marshall Plan credits had found their way to Canada. Canada's exchange crisis dissolved.

The Abbott Plan was tailor-made to deal with the reality that the United States was increasingly running out of resources at the same time as the appetite of its military-industrial complex was voracious. In the Paley Report (1952), of twenty-nine key commodities in which the U.S. was potentially deficient, Canada was cited as the probable major source of supply for twelve — including iron ore, nickel, aluminum, copper, lead, zinc and asbestos — a number of which were critical for the Pentagon; events were subsequently to add oil and gas to the list.

Canadian policy toward the U.S. in the postwar period has been one of increasing dependence not only by incentives to American capital, but also by the diligent pursuit of "special status" within the American empire and a policy of "exemptionalism".[35] The former is evident from the military agreements of World War II to postwar defense production sharing to the autopact; the latter, which amounts to running down to Washington and getting exemptions, is evident from the Interest Equalization Tax of 1963 and U.S. balance of payments directives of 1965 and 1968.

The autopact is of particular interest in any analysis of postwar Canadian industrial policy since the auto industry is by a wide margin the largest employer in the secondary manufacturing sector. The great success of the industry down into the interwar period, in spite of its branch plant character, broke down in the postwar period as Canada's Commonwealth customers emulated Canada in attracting branch plants via high tariffs, and as Germany, Britain, Japan, Sweden, France and Italy offered cars of a type shunned by the U.S. companies in their North American production but with considerable appeal to Canadian buyers. With exports dwindling while imports of parts from the U.S. continued, the Canadian economy faced a steadily widening deficit on automotive account to the point that the Pearson Government in the mid-1960's had to take action. Faced with the choice of radically restructuring the Canadian industry to serve the Canadian , and possibly overseas markets — which probably would have required public ownership as the alternative to foreign private ownership — or restructuring it on continental lines such that imports from the U.S. would be offset by exports to the U.S., not surprisingly the Canadian government pressed the U.S. for the special status that would make the latter option possible. The U.S., not yet facing the full brunt of the dollar crisis that was just around the corner, and seeing the pact as part of a broader package — including Canadian peacekeeping commitments and discouraging Canada from punitive measures against *Time* and *Readers' Digest* — went along.

For the first few years, Canadian production expanded and the deficit closed, though at the same time strategic management decisions were recentralized in Detroit. But with the recent American recession, which was earlier and deeper than the Canadian downturn, the deficit has widened ominously and there is widespread unemployment in the Canadian auto industry. This has created a Canadian clamour to renegotiate the pact so as to provide greater employment safeguards for Canada, while at the same time there is increasing pressure from protectionist elements within the U.S. to renegotiate, if not abrogate, the pact so as to shift jobs from Canada to the United States. It would be difficult to find a clearer example of the risks, and costs, which a small country assumes by letting a major industry fall almost wholly under the control of the corporations of a large country, and then trying, short-sightedly, to minimize the costs by common market-type integration.[36]

A brief look at the key resource industry, oil and gas, shows how Canada, though potentially self-sufficient as a result of major postwar discoveries: has alienated its resources into the hands of the multinationals (indeed, ironically, a major consequence of the great Leduc strike in Alberta in 1947 was that four Canadian-owned oil companies that imported, refined and marketed were taken over by multinationals as they integrated forward from their Alberta discoveries); has made long-term commitments to export as much as half of its oil and gas to the U.S., thereby ruling out an otherwise feasible national policy; is now developing tar sands oil and Arctic gas and oil for domestic markets, the cost of which is much greater than the conventional supplies which are still being shipped to the U.S.; and is on the verge of signing a Treaty with the United States that will guarantee the U.S. a secure pipeline right-of-way across Canada to take Alaskan gas to the lower 48 states — in effect, a modern version of the Panama Canal. None of this is understandable except in the context of the predominance of U.S. ownership of the Canadian oil and gas industry.[37]

How has all of this been reflected in changes in class structure in the postwar period? The study of Wallace Clement shows that: "The economic elite of 1972 is more exclusive in social origins, more upper class and more closely knit by family ties than in 1952."[38] It is this that has happened in the era of special status within the empire of the American-based multinationals.

The question inevitably arises as to whether this strategy can continue to create a prosperous Canada. Hutcheson, after noting that Canada "despite its colonial aspects, has developed into a rich country" adds "This development is now threatened...", and reminds us "The succession of capitalist development by underdevelopment has been a common fate for many regions of capitalist countries, as the history of the Maritimes testifies. In fact, as the example of Argentina may show, this is a fate that can be visited upon whole countries."[39]

Prosperity built on the exploitation of non-renewable resources is inherently risky. Canada is already dotted with ghost towns as forests and mines have given out, and it is not absurd to enquire whether a ghost country is possible. Bourgault[40], in fact, raises the spectre that Canada will become "a resource-based economy (with) no resources". The last relatively untouched frontier, the Canadian Arctic and sub-Arctic, is now almost completely under lease to oil companies and mining companies. The prospects of falling back on manufacturing are not attractive, except in the context of radical re-structuring, for as Bourgault shows, among western countries only Greece and Ireland have a lower percentage of their work force employed in manufacturing than Canada, while Canada heads the list for per capita imports of manufactured goods by a wide margin.

One possible option that exists in principle within the capitalist rules of the game is to make Canada a more effective base for multi-national corporations. By any comparison based on population or

GNP Canada is clearly drastically underrepresented amongst the developed countries in this regard, and particularly relative to the United States. But another Science Council of Canada Study, by Arthur J. Cordell,[41] suggests that it would be difficult, if not impossible, to correct this. After extensive examination of the operations of Canadian-based multinationals, Cordell promulgates as an "iron law": "when a company in a relatively small country expands its international operations into a significantly larger market it finds over time, that it pays to locate not only production but support and managerial functions in the larger offshore market area."

In the face of the apparent decline of U.S. hegemony and the resurgence of inter-imperialist rivalry, it may well be that Canada is backed into a corner, ill-prepared to act and with no easy options.

In principle there are many options; in fact, there are few if any. The most obvious, having gone so far down the road of continental integration, is to go much further. Many conventional economists, led by Harry Johnson, support this option in their advocacy of free trade, but, in fact, it does not appear to be on the political agenda of either the United States or Canada. Canada is clearly interested in bilateral arrangements with the U.S. on an industry-by-industry basis, but has only been able to work out two — defense production sharing and the autopact, and as we have seen, the latter is already problematic for both countries. There is a limited U.S. interest in such arrangements since, in the nature of the case, they tend to benefit Canada; the U.S. stated preference is for less limited and less partial arrangements. But in this century Canada has tended to pull back from across-the-board arrangements, and this remains a reality of Canadian politics.

Another route might be called "greater diversity in dependence". It consists of assiduously courting foreign capital other than from the U.S., for example, Japanese, presumably on the grounds that one country's capital substitutes for the others; in fact, they may be supplementary and additive. Prime Minister Trudeau is presently seeking "a contractual arrangement" with European common market countries, but no-one, Mr. Trudeau included, seems to know what that means and one suspects it is only a nostalgic search for the old North Atlantic triangle.

Canada has been more willing than the U.S. throughout the postwar period to trade with Communist countries, notably the Peoples Republic of China and Cuba. But trade in manufactured goods has quickly come up against the extraterritorial extension to America-controlled subsidiaries of U.S. law. The U.S. has recently moved to relax those restrictions on trade with the "enemy" but has done so as part of detente where its companies can themselves trade.

Imbedded therein is a deeper problem that inhibits the Canadian interest in a more profitable arrangement with the Third World in terms of both trade and investment. Our firms are mostly merely subsidiaries of U.S. firms and our manufactured goods the same, but higher-cost.

The sub-imperial strategy seems to have been a once-and-for-all historial phenomenon.

Unless the United States, then, can continue to afford special status for Canada, and the evidence runs to the contrary, [42] contradictions are likely to become more evident within the Canadian political economy. Both unilateral American action and excessive selling-off of Canadian resources have historically risked a nationalist backlash within Canada.

There is — indeed, there has been for some time — some evidence of this in Canada. The great postwar surge in foreign investment was followed by the bourgeois nationalism of Diefenbaker, Coyne and Gordon in the late 1950's, while U.S. balance of payments directives in the 1960's converted Eric Kierans from internationalism to nationalism. By the early '70's there was some legislative payoff. The Canada Development Corporation was created, initially using public funds and wholly-government owned, but expected to go public shortly. Some existing Crown corporations were turned over to it, and it began to acquire other interests. The acquisitions to date have been a mixed bag, varying from the spectacular take-over of U.S. Texasgulf, that is, a take-over of foreign capital by domestic capital, to minority participation in the American-dominated Arctic Gas consortium which proposes to move Alaskan and Mackenzie Delta gas down the Mackenzie Valley, primarily for American markets.

Throughout the post-1957 period there has been a gradual process of defining certain sectors as key sectors where Canadian control must predominate. Given the character of the Canadian capitalist class, these key sectors have turned out to be those in which the traditional elite operates — banks, trust companies, insurance companies, newspapers, radio and television. Uranium was added for national security reasons at least to the extent of blocking an attempted U.S. take-over of Denison Mines. In the federal election campaign last year the reigning Liberals talked about greater Canadian participation in future resource developments, but there is no evidence that the full protection of the key sector approach is about to be applied even to future developments, much less any intent to begin the massive rollback that would be necessary to repatriate this sector. The whole area of publishing is currently under scrutiny, and only very recently the Government finally moved against the special tax privileges of *Time* and *Readers' Digest*, and at least the Canadian edition of *Time* seems doomed.

After no less than three government reports on foreign ownership — the Watkins Report, the Wahn Report and the Gray Report — in 1973 the Government finally created a Foreign Investment Review Agency. To date its powers are limited to screening take-overs, and have yet to be extended to the setting up of new subsidiaries. It has approved the great majority —, leading its left critics to compare it to having a referee at a rape — and no matter what its decision, it typically gives no reason for it. The Government ignored the clear advice of the Gray Report that, given the extent of foreign ownership, the screening mechanism must have power to screen the activities of existing firms. Nevertheless, it is a reasonable presumption that the age-old process of foreign take-over of Canadian companies is now, through regulation, creating greater benefit, or less cost, than before.

All of this does not really add up to very much. Nationalist sentiment exists throughout Canada but its mobilization for the working out of new and different strategies, particularly with respect to industrial policy, is difficult. Nationalism, as is evident from this paper, has no firm roots in the Canadian business class, and hence has little legitimacy within the two major political parties, both of which are business-supported. Nationalism is problematic for the working class because its organized sections are substantially within so-called international unions which are really American unions operating in Canada. Canadian social democracy, as an alternative to the explicitly pro-business political parties, has its roots not only in American Gomperism but also in British Fabianism, and neither of these ideologies is anti-imperialist; hence, even Canada's social democratic party is not nationalist.[43]

It follows that the "best" that can be expected is that diffuse nationalist pressure on the state from the electorate — which must periodically be consulted — complements specific day-to-day pressures from vested business interests to lead to half-hearted moves to state capitalism. In practice that may mean simply the use of public monies to shore up private projects, which in turn may amount to public subsidizing of foreign capital, as would appear to be the case in the recent Syncrude oil sands deal in Alberta. It is a moot point whether this may not, in the long-run, feed rather than coopt nationalist sentiment.

The contradictions in the Canadian political economy may well be deep and deepening, and if that is the case, the means for resolving them are, to say the least, unclear. If foreign investment increases beyond some point, it tends to become irreversible, not only because of the foreign-controlled companies' control of market shares and of surplus for future growth, but also because the capacity of the state as a countervailing force is hopelessly compromised.

But it does seem clear that "industrial policy" that amounts to only marginal changes to a truncated industrial structure that is controlled by powerful multinational corporations will be of slight avail. It is analagous to advocating Keynesian fine-tuning as the capitalist economies skate close to the brink of a Great Crash. Economics as conventionally conceived, and hence the economic policy that flows from it, seems to be of limited value. The obstacles to a rational industrial policy for Canada will not be identified by confining oneself to conventional economic analysis, for Canada's present industrial structure cannot be "explained" without recourse to factors that economists deliberately neglect as "non-economic".

If economics is to be useful it must become again political economy. We must grapple with the reality that the industrial structure is imbeded in the class structure. We must admit of the possibility, when dealing with a dependent capitalist economy such as Canada's, that the state may be an obstacle to indigenous industrialization, and not a neutral entity to which economists can offer prescriptions framed in innocence. And just as marginalist policies flow from conventional economics, the "policies" that would flow from political economy would be fundamentally political, that is, changes in the distribution of power or in the class structure.

NOTES

*   I am indebted to Mr. Jose Serra of Cornell University for his helpful comments on our earlier draft of this paper.
(1)   The basic theme of this paper draws heavily on the historical research, mostly still unpublished, of Professor R.T. Naylor of McGill University; see, however, his "The rise and fall of the third commercial empire of the St. Lawrence" in Gary Teeple (ed.), *Capitalism and the national question in Canada* (Toronto, 1972) and "The History of Domestic and Foreign Capital in Canada" in Robert M. Laxer (ed.), *(Canada) Ltd: The Political Economy of Dependency* (Toronto, 1973).
(2)   Jim Laxer, "Introduction to the Political Economy of Canada" *(Canada) Ltd.,* p. 26.
(3)   This is argued at greater length in my "A Staple Theory of Economic Growth", *Canadian Journal of Economics and Political Science,* May 1963; reprinted in W.T. Easterbrook and M.H. Watkins (eds.) *Approaches to Canadian Economic History,* (Toronto, 1967). For a later version of the staple theory cast less in terms of conventional economics and more in terms of Marxist analysis, see my "Resources and Underdevelopment" in *(Canada) Ltd.*
(4)   John Hutcheson, "The Capitalist State in Canada" in *(Canada) Ltd.*
(5)   Naylor, "The rise and fall of...", *op. cit.,* p. 2. The objection may be made, with good reason, that any inference that Canada is presently an underdeveloped country, given its standard of living from a global perspective, must be rejected. The world does not merely consist of developed and underdeveloped countries but of a broad spectrum; Canada might be characterized as a dependent developed country from the perspective of the level of per capita income, or as a rich underdeveloped country from the perspective of the structure of the economy.
(6)   Naylor, "The History of Foreign and Domestic Capital in Canada", *op. cit.,* pp. 44-45.
(7)   Naylor, "The rise and fall of...", *op. cit.,* p. 3.
(8)   Wallace Clement, *The Canadian Corporate Elite: An Analysis of Economic Power,* (Toronto, 1975), p. 32. Clement's historical analysis is based on Naylor's work, yet he is, incredibly, able to write with respect to contemporary Canada: "the Canadian economy remains controlled in large part by a set of families who have been in the past and still remain at the core of the Canadian economy" (p. 150). Again, he writes that the split between the commercial and industrial capitalist classes, about which he has learned from Naylor, not only "does not mean the total bourgeoisie is not powerful — indeed, it may be more powerful because of the continental context" (p. 355). In a world which is dominated by giant corporations operating in industry and resources, and in which Canada has an extremely high level of foreign control, Clement, who is a sociologist, seems to be grasping at what, to a non-sociologist, is self-evidently mere straw. Contrast Clement with Naylor: "The independent sector of the Canadian bourgeoisie, largely the descendants of merchant capital, is small in relation to the total. Control of the Canadian economy lies overwhelmingly with the branch plant group." ("The rise and fall of...", p. 33).
(9)   This perspective on Marx draws both from Wallace Clement, *ibid,* and from Gary Teeple, "Land, labour, and capital in pre-Confederation Canada" in *Capitalism and the national question in Canada.*
(10)   Paul Baran, *The Political Economy of Growth,* (New York, 1957).
(11)   Andre Gunder Frank, "The Development of Underdevelopment", *Monthly Review,* 1966; reprinted in Frank, *Latin America: Underdevelopment or Revolution,* (New York, 1969).
(12)   Naylor, "The rise and fall of...", p. 31.
(13)   Harry Magdoff and Paul M. Sweezy, "Notes on the Multinational Corporation", *Monthly Review,* October 1969.
(14)   See Naylor, "The History of Foreign and Domestic Capital" for a discussion of the much-neglected phenomenon of surplus appropriation from the Quebecois peasants and artisans by the British (including Albany) merchants and contractors who rushed in after 1760.
(15)   Patents and bonussing as important parts of the National Policy have tended to be neglected, except by Naylor.
(16)   On the "Little National Policy" of Ontario, see H.V. Nelles, *The Politics of Development: Forests, Mines and Hydro-Electric Power in Ontario, 1849-1941,* (Toronto, 1974).
(17)   Glen Williams, "Canadian Industrialization: We Ain't Growin' Nowhere", *This Magazine,* March-April 1975.

(18) Andre Gunder Frank, *Capitalism and Under-development in Latin America,* (New York, 1959).
(19) Naylor, "The rise and fall of...", p. 2.
(20) See Jim Laxer, "Canadian Manufacturing and U.S. Trade Policy" in *(Canada) Ltd.*
(21) Naylor, "The rise and fall of...", p. 35.
(22) A contemporary version of "Canada as imperialist" is to cite the role of Canadian based resource companies such as Alcan, Inco and Falconbridge in the Third World; but Falconbrige is unambiguously U.S. — controlled (by Superior Oil through McIntyre Mines) and, statistics on Canadian shareholding not-withstanding, Alcan and Inco may be as well through blocks of shares held in the U.S. For a useful discussion of this, see Jack Warnock, "Canadian Sub-Imperialism? A Reply", *This Magazine,* March-April 1975. This is not, of course, to deny that there is genuine Canadian direct investment (Massey-Ferguson, Brascan, Moore Corporation, the banks, Weston, Noranda) but rather to suggest the propriety over-all of the term "North America" as used by Third World countries.
(23) Eric Kierans, *Report on Natural Resources Policy in Manitoba,* (Manitoba, 1973), p. 37.
(24) H. Marshall, F.A. Southard and K.W. Taylor, *Canadian-American Industry: A Study in International Investment,* (Toronto, 1936).
(25) This writer is in the early stages of a study of this nature.
(26) See in particular O.W. Main, *The Canadian Nickel Industry,* (Toronto, 1955) and Nelles, *The Politics of Development, op. cit.;* the following account draws heavily on the latter, which draws in turn on Main.
(27) Pierre L. Bourgault, *Innovation and the Structure of Canadian Industry,* (Ottawa, 1972), p. 51.
(28) Marshall, Southard and Taylor, *op. cit.*
(29) George Grant, *Lament for a Nation: The Defeat of Canadian Nationalism* (Toronto, 1965), pp. 9-10.
(30) Donald Creighton, *Towards the discovery of Canada.*
(31) The most notorious of these transactions was the sale of the Victory Aircraft plant at Malton, Ontario to A.V. Rœ of Britain, and of the Canadair Plant at Montreal to General Dynamics of the U.S. at bargain basement prices; in the latter case, journalist Peter Newman states that the plant was built for $22 million and sold for $4 million (Letter to author, November 15, 1973).
(32) David Wolfe, *Political Culture, Economic Policy and the Growth of Foreign Investment in Canada, 1945 to 1957,* M.A. thesis, Carleton University, Ottawa, 1973; the following two paragraphs draw from that thesis.
(33) J. Grant Glassco, *Certain Aspects of Taxation Relating to Investment in Canada by Non-Residents,* A Study done for the Royal Commission on Canada's Economic Prospects, (Ottawa, 1957).
(34) Just as Ontario had a "Little National Policy" in the late 19th and early 20th centuries, so too in this period it joined in the program of corporate welfare and got the lion's share of the branch plants. See Glen Williams, *The Ontario Department of Trade and Development: A Case Study of Capitalist Public Policy in Relation to Industrial Growth,* M.A. thesis, York University, Toronto, 197). Williams reminds us that "the most important function of government in a capitalist society is to create a political climate suitable for the unobstructed expansion of economic growth", and that this meant, for Canada and Ontario, not only providing services and subsidies to the corporations, but deflecting potential public hostility away from foreign capital. The rhetoric of the Cold War was, of course, the key to legitimizing the decisive leap forward in the U.S. takeover of Canada, but flashy programs geared to elections also had their place, and the latter were to become an Ontario specialty.
(35) The term is used by R.D. Cuff and J.L. Granatstein in "Canada and the Perils of 'Exemptionalism'", *Queen's Quarterly,* No. 4, 1972.
(36) For a capsule history of the Canadian auto industry, see Jim Laxer, "Canadian Manufacturing and U.S. Trade Policy", *(Canada) Ltd.;* he has a book-length study now in progress.
(37) For a fuller discussion of Canada's oil and gas industry with particular reference to recent developments, see James Laxer, *Canada's Energy Crisis* (Toronto, 1974).
(38) "Foreward" by John Porter in Clement, *op. cit.,* p. xi.
(39) Hutcheson, *op. cit.,* pp. 166-167.
(40) Bourgault, *op. cit.*
(41) Arthur J. Cordell, *The Multinational Firm, Foreign Direct Investment, and Canadian Science Policy* (Ottawa, 1972).

(42) Nixon's new economic policies of August 15, 1971 to stop the floodtide against the U.S. dollar included a temporary surcharge on imports; Canada was not exempt and this time, in spite of the normal begging mission to Washington, no exemption was granted. In April 1972, President Nixon, in an address to a joint session of the Houses of Parliament spelled out the Nixon Doctrine for Canada when he unilaterally declared Canada independent. There have been no further grants of special status or exemptions, and a roll-back of those previously granted is, as noted with respect to the autopact, a possibility.

(43) For a lengthier presentation of this argument, see my "Trade Unions in Canada" in *(Canada) Ltd.*

WORLD INEQUALITY:
political aspects

THE CURRENT ROLE OF THE NATION-STATE

Jean Piel

THE problem of the State in its classical form begins with Rome and Caesar. In Rome, for the first time, there comes into being a system of power, rooted within a territory, unique in character and claiming to encompass everything.

When this power wanes, decomposes and disintegrates, with no Caesar to reestablish the principle of unity on earth, successors and inheritors of the Empire have no alternative but to idealize this aspiration for unity through the substitution of God for Caesar. Thus the fall of Rome paved the way for a militant church empowered to conquer or reconquer, be it spiritually, Barbarians and slaves.

The successor to the territorial power, rooted in the Empire and in time, the *state* is the heavenly eternal power, God. Both claim to be *unique* and *total*.

However, for two millenia this assertion has confronted insuperable obstacles. Rome was not the universe and the Christian population certainly did not encompass the whole of humanity. Materialistic or spiritual imperialism has had to learn to live within its limits. Externally, there remained always barbarian Kingdoms and gentiles to be conquered or contained. Internally, the dialectic of social exploitation constantly gave birth to new internal barbarians. From those two sources, new centrifugal aspirations for power emerged and eventually destroyed the unity achieved, or sought, by the Church or by the Empire.

Moreover, peripheral to the state with its vested power exerted on populations bound to territories, and favored by its existence either at its edges, or inside it, there existed another source of power based on the *exchange* of goods, ideas, persons, i.e., on the *market*.

To territorial power, hierarchical, visible, responsible for demarcated populations, corresponded an opposed extra-territorial power, diffused, hidden, anonymous, ubiquitous and not tied to any land. Senators stood opposed to horsemen, the gods of the Roman pantheon to eastern cults and to the early Christians, the legions of Caesar to the homeless slaves of Spartacus, the Imperial state to the network of complicity and solidarity of seamen-merchants who traded with the East.

Thus, at the level of the formal descriptive analysis of the original evolution of State power, one notes the permanent *tension* between two sources of power, at the same time complementary and in conflict: a territorial power, visible to the population it dominated and from whom it extorted surplus product.

The other extra-territorial power, scarcely visible, was for the most part hidden from most peoples. This power was founded upon the exchange of goods and ideas produced by peoples under the control of the Imperial State or its inheritors.

The whole story of state power in universal history is contained in these two sets of mythical extremes. On the one hand, a territorial power supposed to be the sole master of its production and of its internal and external exchanges: this is the case of the Inca Empire as analyzed by Louis Baudin; or of the medieval manorial fief, until it became necessary to reconquer the Grail. On the other hand, a mercantile power, financial or spiritual, such as that of the Phoenicians, the Jewish *diaspora*, the various Gnostic sects or, closer to us, the "Trotskyist plot."

In this more or less closed system, where state and anti-state tendencies alternate without ever gaining full control despite the numerous attempts to restore the imperial order (Carolingian, Romano-Germanic, Byzantine, etc.) up to the final failure confirmed by the fall of Constantinople, two moments of rupture brought about a radical transformation of the power structure in the Western world. These two turning points reflect a higher stage in the growth of western societies in the evolution towards nation-state.

The first event took place during the Middle Ages when, on the debris of the imperial order, an alliance of the feudal seignors and the Church led to the creation of dynastic families who took root in the various regions of the Christian universe and founded what would become the *territorial state*.

The second event was the so-called modern era, when on the basis of preceding tradition, monarchical families, still allied to but in conflict with the Church, eventually achieved the unification of their peoples, thereby creating the conditions for the establishment of the *nation-state*. These two events constitute definite departures from the former imperial ideal in that the new state forewent the ideals of uniqueness and universality. They had no equivalent to this period of universal history, since neither China nor India nor Islam experienced similar transformations. It was thus an important event when the West — or Europe — took the historical initiative in terms of inventing forms of power and social life.

It was during the 10th century when, for the first time, the Church renounced its hopes to recreate the formal political unity of the West deriving from Caesar. In France, for example, it encouraged regional initiatives, particularly those of the Capetians as evidenced by the legendary alliance between Louis VI and Suger. With the advent of duchies, earldoms, and kingdoms, the various would-be European nations progressively took shape. The times were marked by a passage from the *military state* based upon the success of a handful of adventurers and conquerors who could achieve timely alliances with the bishops and monks, to the *territorial state* which thereupon asserted its sedentary durability. Under the military protection and control of their feudal and monarchical elites, the peoples could hope for some measure of stability, internal fusion, and durability. The church alone maintained a central organization and an ideology which preserved the Roman legacy despite nascent, albeit growing "national" differentiations.

However, the *territorial stage*, was caught between peoples who were difficult to mobilize for its defense, the Church, and the merchants, and lived for a long time in a state of precarious equilibrium. Its access to human and material resources was contested by local lords often in close association with the "homeless" merchants. Its access to men and to souls was disputed by the Church which monopolized education and ideological conditioning. Its access to territory was constantly frustrated by neighbouring territorial states themselves, in turn threatening and threatened, for identical reasons.

From this evil some good was to come. Constantly threatened, the dynastic territorial state had to improve its defensive and offensive capabilities of violence, at first military and financial, later ideological. Always on the verge of bankruptcy, the state allied itself with the bourgeoisie and the free cities against the Church and the feudal lords, thereby "popularizing" its power, sinking roots in the "nation." The state became "national." Lacking the traditional legitimacy which it lost as it began to violate the rules of the game, it progressively utilized Roman Law, when necessary heretical tendencies of thought arose, and even created "national" Churches.

Thus the territorial state slowly became a pre-national state by secularizing social life and appropriating part of the Roman legacy: the Roman Law, the revival of the market, but this time on the basis of rural or urban small communities, reconstituted between the 10th and 15th centuries, and through the resurgence of arts, culture and philosophy. After a phase of virtually mandatory autarchic withdrawal, the universal contacts that had characterized the West were renewed. The nation-state was born from this emerging pattern of exchange and dialogue between the territorial state and the rest of the world, particularly its non-Christian part.

It is not by accident that the nation-state was consolidated in the modern era by the very process of conquering parts of the non-European world. In the 16th century, the consolidation of national monarchies rested upon the discovery and the conquest of the Americas, i.e., upon the expansion of the mercantile market and the pre-capitalist techniques of production that sustained it in the New World. During the 19th century, the consolidation of European and North American nations, sustained as it was by triumphant industrial capitalism, had corollary colonial expansion and rivalry, including in areas of ancient and/or powerful state-based civilizations (India, Japan, China, Middle East, etc.). It seemed as if, unable to reestablish its internal imperial unity (as evidenced by the failure of Napoleon), the West renewed its tradition of external imperial expansion through the nation-state. After having appropriated Rome's philosophy and its legal heritage in opposition to the Church from the 15th to the 18th century, the nation-state finally adopted its imperial tradition, albeit in an exclusivist pattern that necessarily led to confrontation with neighbouring nation-states. The imperialism of the contemporary nation-state has as a corollary inter-state imperial conflicts. Thus it becomes impossible to reconstitute the initial imperial unity from which, in terms of the form and structure of power, Western macro-society arose. Divided among themselves by their external conquests, the nation-states were condemned to fight each other in world wars. Imperialism resulted in the exacerbation of nationalism within the dominant nation-states.

This explains to what extent, in the modern era, the nascent or consolidated nation-state is such a powerful agent of transformation of the rest of the world. It is under its control, if not in fact due to its initiative, that new lands, their people and their resources, are integrated into the market which thereby takes on the character of universality. It is under its military protection that entire peoples are brought to heel, bit by bit, often violently and submitted to new modes of production, new patterns of consumption, new systems of belief and thought. This epic of the expansion of the forces of production of triumphant capitalism — for it was an epic, in its dimensions, its brutality and its importance — has been often enough described, exalted and denounced. Let us note however that it has been conceived, willed and executed by political and economic power groups which were not necessarily linked at the outset to the bureaucracies of the nation apparatus — slave-traders, merchant-adventurers, pirates and buccaneers, merchant-bankers, seamen, and soldiers of fortune — but it was progressively taken over by the nation-states which found it to their advantage ultimately to become the agents and the guarantors of this colonial and imperial expansion. However brutal, from the 16th to the 19th century the nation-state strongly contributed to the *progress* of one mode of production. It strongly contributed to destroying the *status quo* in which non-Western societies tended to become crystallized, as they came to feel they were losing historical initiative in this period. In turn, this transformation was imposed in such an aggressive way that it condemned for a long span of history such dominated social formations to asserting their identity vis-à-vis the imperialist West only in purely messianic, passive or subserviently imitative ways. For "peripheral" social formations, the compulsory challenge of a dominating capitalist mode of production was dearly paid for by the pitiless exploitation of people and resources and by preventive for sometime of any real and effective historical initiative of their own. Peripheral humanity was condemned, for a long time, to be merely the reserve of the Western nation-state. Though the latter initially served to transform this humanity by means of colonial or imperial expansion, it rapidly revealed itself to be primarily an exploiter, and in the end a staunchly conservative force. Once the partition of the world was complete, the chauvinist-imperialist state could only think about maintaining the *status quo* within its sphere of influence. A competitive connivance was established among the imperial nation-states that lasted up to 1914.

Internally, the nation-state, at least until the first World War, also played a role in transforming the social strata it dominated, created or controlled. One could summarize the development by saying that as the ruling group which initially obtained control of an inhabited area stabilized it tended to transform client or community social relationships into class relations, by the very dynamic involved in the exercise of the institutionalized violence of state power. A permanent share of the territorial group's surplus was absorbed by the elite which used it to reproduce and expand the social hierarchy that assured the whole group of possession of its territory. In extending itself, this power to control the expanded reproduction became lasting and strong in virtue of its tacit acceptance, by the producers whether voluntary or coerced. When this process spreads beyond territorial groups that are limited in number and area — the tribe, the chiefdom, the fief — to the level of geo-political regions that are well integrated under the authority and initiative of a stable power group, all the necessary conditions are present for the appearance of class conflicts within the national state.

From thereon, facing a ruling class still legitimized by the initiative taken by the founding ancestors in their conquest of territorial power the requirements of the exercise of state powers made it necessary to multiply "intermediate groups" which entered rapidly in to conflict with the mass of producers, whom they exploit, as well as with the aristocrats, who have become more and more useless and parasitic. The "nation" thus became aware of itself, of its autonomous existence vis-à-vis the old dynastic state. It freed itself and founded thereby, against the monarchical territorial state, a national state constituted by those representing the general interest. This was at least the general tendency which was characterized in its most complete form by the French Revolution.

The depersonalized state became the pawn of opposing factions who, in order to win the contest, did not hesitate to mobilize those who would normally never be consulted, i.e., the agents of material production and reproduction of the system, the people. Mobilized and sensitized, the people realized that the nation-state, for which they were being asked to fight, did not belong to them, and was a major factor in keeping them dominated and exploited. The proletarians discovered they had no "homeland." In a world where the effective model of social organization was the nation-state, they longed to conquer it for themselves, and not follow the bourgeois or feudal model. In this struggle, they could count on the historical legacy which the ruling classes had instilled in them, often forcibly and without them knowing it: ethnic-linguistic identification with their fellow countrymen and their land; anthropological — professional identification with their class-brothers across regional and racial frontiers. In the same thrust that led them to challenge the bourgeoisie and ruling classes in their control of the national state, the proletarian, the producer — with their ally, the intellectual who has not fallen prey to the system of domination and ideological conformity — discovered as complementary variables internationalism and their own national character. In this awakening of consciousness, the nation-state was the stake as well as the indispensable catalyzer, forcing the class struggle to achieve its only solution that is the seizure and the destruction of state power and its replacement by a new social and political order, functioning on principles that would ensure a transitory violent dictatorship of a coalition of popular forces to complete the elimination of the former order, and, in case the project succeeded, to manage for the majority the most complete possibilities of life, either within the framework of the nation or within a supranational framework which largely remains to be devised.

By its internal dynamics, the nation-state is historically the first form of social power and, for the time being, the principal if not the only one capable of transforming the society it creates and which creates it, until it transcends itself through revolution. The state, historically created by exclusive and dominating power groups in order to institute and perpetuate their own pre-eminence, developed a class structure and dynamic which leads to its own destruction.

This is so, provided it can find the determination within itself and in conjunction with what goes on in other nation-states (the problem of revolutionary internationalism).

Let us start with some facts. Since the end of the 19th century, the great social, modernizing transformations, revolutionary or radical, that have taken place, were achieved not through external pressure but from within society, possessing *two* essential characteristics.

These transformations have been conceived and carried out, utilizing and opposing the most advanced economic, social, intellectual ideas of their time and elaborated from foreign and/or international practice.

These transformations all have had the nation-state as their initiator or framework and in all cases, it was their essential means as well as their goal, definitive or transitory.

As early as the 18th century this was true of Peter the Great's Russia or of the insurgent colonies which were to constitute the United States of America. In the 19th century, it was true of Meiji Japan. In the 20th century, it applied to revolutionary Russia and to China, to the Arab-African world, to South-East Asia, Cuba, and Vietnam. Wherever new forces seek to transform their society, it is within the national and state framework that they operate. In the middle of the 19th century, Marx and Engels had already acknowledged this trait with regard to the European revolution in the *Communist Manifesto*.

One might of course argue that some of the examples are taken from situations where the essential motivation was the liberation of the social group concerned, confronted with foreign, colonial or imperialist occupation. We shall thus examine cases at the turn of the two last centuries in which no one can deny that the initiative belonged to reformers or revolutionaries concerned, not with liberation, but with voluntary *transformation* of the state and the nation.

In Meiji Japan, the economic and social revolution, with its modernizing and capitalist character, was conceived and executed at the highest state level, by the emperor, in order to change the state apparatus itself. This "revolution" was thus national and state-controlled from A to Z. In Lenin's Russia, Bolshevik leaders had stressed at a very early stage the necessary theoretical links that exist between the *state and revolution*.

In this latter case, however, a de facto contradiction, consequently a theoretical one, complicated the question, one which all revolutionaries in imperialist states have had to face in the first half of the 20th century. This ambiguity stemmed from the fact that the state which the Bolsheviks wanted to destroy and transform was not a national state but an imperial state which dominated numerous and disparate ethno-territorial groups, many of which could scarcely be considered nations. However, the revolutionary forces, essentially pan-Russian, initially operated and triumphed only within a national framework. What status would the victorious, new masters of the Russian national state apparatus accord to the other populations of the empire as well as to the imperial institutions of the conquered state apparatus?

Therein doubtless lay the historical genius of Lenin, Stalin and their colleagues: they opted for the extension of the nation-state model to the social groups theretofore dominated, proclaimed their right to secession from the dominant Russian nation-state, while vigorously striving to get all these nation-states, new and old, heirs of the Tsarist empire, to federate in a single union of Socialist Republics, organized on the Soviet model. Put to the test under extreme stress, as we know, during the Second World War, the structure held firm and revealed a hitherto unheard of phenomenon in contemporary history: a multinational patriotism capable of sacrificing 18 million persons of every ethno-national group on the fields of battle.

One could argue that the United States of America was also born out of a federative free consensus among equal and sovereign territorial states. However, not only were coloured minorities excluded (especially Black slaves) but also, despite minor nuances, all the states were truly equal. In this new country, devoid of a centralizing tradition, Pennsylvania was not colonizing Virginia. The relationship between Russia and Kazakstan around 1920 was quite different.

For some thirty years, Soviet successes in the incomplete, dramatic but unprecedentedly rapid transformation not only of Russian society but also of the Empire's former minorities, weighed heavily in the mind of revolutionaries in other countries. The Soviet model alone could be imagined, and no other revolutionary perspective existed except that of some federal union between freely associated states — as for example the French Union established following World War II. But the geographic, economic and political conditions were not the same; moreover, imperialist forces, enlightened by experience, tried to forestall developments, either by creating themselves the new imperial formations (Commonwealth, French

Union) or eventually by acceding to mounting national aspirations. These aspirations were to be directed by *leaders* sufficiently honest and sincere to be credible in the eyes of their own people, and also sufficiently identified with liberal ideology so as not to call into question the principles of foreign economic dependence and internal social hierarchy that served as the basis of the existence of an imperialist market.

Between these two approaches, only a few *leaders* stubbornly pursued their quest for another road, anti-imperialist, national, and revolutionary. Among them, the Mao in China, and Ho-Chi-Minh in Vietnam. Their tenacity and, finally, their victory has had a considerable impact on the rest of the colonized peoples. Among the *leaders* of the oppressed countries of Asia, Africa and Latin America, it has accelerated the realization that the claim of immediate independence, here and now, made against the imperial metropole, was the quickest way to foster mobilization and rapid transformation of their archaic societies. They relinquished the hope of seeing revolution occur first in the metropole which would subsequently grant them nationhood, as happened in the USSR at the beginning of the century. They now took the leadership of the nationalist movements calling for an independent state.

This new consciousness, worldwide, became apparent at the first Bandung international conference which assembled the *leaders* of present or former colonies. It was also to be found in the documents of Communist parties, particularly around the 20th Congress of the Soviet C.P., which identified the national liberation movements of the people against imperialism as one of the two main progressive forces of our time. Unfortunately — at least, so it seemed — the traditional ruling classes of the imperialist metropole seemed to realize more rapidly than progressive forces the advantage they could reap from this new situation. After a bloody and obstinate defense of their imperial privileges, they gave in and accepted the inevitable wherever it became inevitable, as in Cuba, Vietnam, Algeria. Indeed, the old imperialist powers agreed to redefine globally their relationships with their former colonies who all obtained the status of nation-states with all the consequences which follow for the transformation of the international situation, the effects of which we have not yet been able to fully assess.

Once again, the nation-state, now the new nations recently catapulted into existence over the debris of colonial empires, played a major role in the transformation of the international balance of power. After Europe and America in the 19th century, Africa and Asia now were organizing as nation-states which would determine their future progress and their international role.

What did the possibility of developing their future history within the framework of the nation-state offer to the former colonies of Latin America, Africa and Asia? In many cases, we are reduced to hypotheses about the future. However, over the last 150 years, one area has experienced the use of the nation-state as a mechanism to overcome an initial colonial situation — Latin America. What do we find there?

Far from promoting real independence — economic, political, diplomatic, technological, cultural — and social progress, the state has more often than not prevented society's democratization in favour of a landowning and financial oligarchy, preventing huge masses of people from really integrating the nation (Indians, Blacks, Metis, poor peasants). The state has in fact assisted international financial and commercial capital to take over whole sectors of these countries' economies.

It is thanks to the state that local aristocracies have prospered at the expense of public finances and of the population, and have been able to take over a society formerly dominated directly by the Iberian powers. Within Latin-American oligarchies, most fortunes or careers have been made through the state, through contract and adjudication, or as provider of political, military and diplomatic careers. In control of a territorial space and a population treated as children, the state has not truly been national, unless one is willing to consider as a "nation" the approximately 40 oligarchic creole families who possessed all the wealth and all the power in each of these countries.

The Latin-American example proves precisely that, from a revolutionary point of view, or even from merely a progressive point of view, the nation-state in formerly colonized countries is no panacea. The "nation-state", in the spirit of its founders, had as a minimum to become a truly *national* state, i.e. the business of all citizens equal in law and in the market. For it is within an expanding world of free trade capitalism and liberal legislation that the contemporary nation-state was born. Where the conditions of expansion of this market had not altered radically the local relations of production in a true capitalist direction, the pretense to imitate the Western nation-state was bound to fail or to create a neo-colonial caricature. Furthermore, the majority of Asian and African peoples could not even have aspired to this model, as they were directly colonized, without appeal.

What then were the new conditions which enabled these peoples who have just achieved independence as nation-states, to hope to do better in Africa and in Asia than what had been achieved in Latin-America until the middle of the 20th century?

First of all, the rupture in Russia in 1917, proved to the world, that it was possible to break the imperialist chain by mobilizing the masses on behalf of their aspirations, and this in the worst possible conditions of isolation. This break promoted rapid, fundamental structural progress, while having continuously to avoid external intervention.

Second, there was the solidarity between former colonies and a growing awareness among their elites of the major trump cards they held. The former colonies constituted together two-thirds of the land area and four-fifths of the world's population.

Third, there were the contradictions between older and newer imperial metropoles which led them to take or reaffirm more reasonable positions concerning a more just and equalitarian organization of the world's nations.

Fourth, and probably most important, there was the ever present risk of seeing the masses, (at times close to starvation and having nothing to lose, but also no longer isolated culturally as had been the case until around 1950,) realize the contradiction between their misery and their strength and upset the rules of the game abruptly without consultation, not even with their own national leaders. As is well known, fear is often the beginning of wisdom, and both the former imperial governments and the leaders of the new states had thus a common stake in mutual understanding to engage in timely transformation rather than in preservation of the status quo.

The situation was thus no longer that of the states of 19th century Latin-America. The new nation-states had to intervene more and more in favour of progressive, radical or revolutionary transformations.

But would they be capable of doing so? And what would be the tool best adapted to this situation?

One should start by observing that, in the world as it is, where most former colonized people have opted for a national and state development formula, it is hard to envisage an alternative. Return to former colonial empires? Impossible. More discrete forms of imperialism, for example diplomatic and financial? But the "American empire" itself is in crisis, even in what has been for a long time its private hunting ground, Latin-America. And it is two tiny states that have held it in check for the last ten years, one diplomatically, the other militarily: Cuba and Vietnam. There is every reason to believe that, at least in the middle run, the nation-state will keep on being for these states the framework, the means of their people's struggle on the path to real independence externally, and true social and economic development internally.

The state formula for a society is the only one that enables them to train the elites that they still lack — modern technicians and managerial elites, without falling prey to the huge extra-territorial imperialist economic empires which the largely U.S.-controlled multinationals often are. The state formula of managing society is the only one in which it becomes a systematic obligation to integrate fragmented and divided societies into a unified, coherent whole, capable of self-identification and resistance to external aggression. The state formula is the only one which, being readily visible to the emerging nation and rooted in a territory, must at one stage or another account to its people for its behaviour. It is the only institution which in the foreseeable future can mobilize popular masses, in the countries liberated from imperial dependence.

Furthermore, the national and state formula may still have a role to play in solving conflicts which plague economically advanced metropoles. We shall refrain from raising the issue of Québec as we are not too familiar with it. However, we feel compelled to acknowledge that in Québec and in Ireland, for example, patterns of exploitation, domination and regional dependence are being denounced by some political groups who evoke the national formula as being the best means for progressive or revolutionary transformation of the situation.

On the other hand, despite the identity and motivational crises which people like to talk about in the West, one has to admit that it is around the concept of the state or the nation, transcending class or party struggles, that some politicians have attempted to define "new frontiers," a "grand design" in the hope of offering a new perspective to their action. The state was designed, in the light of the crisis experienced by the former imperial system, to mobilize once again the energies of the young elites of these countries. There is much mystification in this. Nonetheless, the classical nation-state, by reinforcing over the last twelve years its organic ties with major national financial and industrial forces, has proven to be a powerful agent of transformation of capitalist structures, within and without the country. Even Spain, for a long time considered the model of inertia, has seen in the last few years a rapid transformation of certain sectors of its economy, through the initiative of multinational corporations as well as of some state technocratic and financial institutions, linked to big business.

It would therefore be an error to believe that the national state is purely and simply an antiquated relic. As the apparatus of institutionalized class violence, in a system of coexistence and confrontation between countries and groups of countries with differing social options, the state is still an essential institution. What is new is that the nation-state is no longer merely a "Western" concept. It is now universal, a phenomenon in expansion.

For some it is a stage in the liberation from a previous colonial situation. For others, the state represents a means to maintain the essence of the status quo nationally as well as regionally and in the world-system, provided they agree to sectorial structural reforms, which are inevitable. Finally for others the state is a means for a terrible struggle not only against unequal development but also for the revolutionary transformation of their society and the world.

Those with this point of view are the progenitors of change in the whole system, who force the others to change in turn either in accordance with their own principles or out of sheer fear. If they remain closely linked with their peoples and with other progressive forces throughout the world, they will retain the principal historical initiative, and continue to be the motor of the present stage of history, thus forcing the last-ditch defenders of imperialism, old and new, to fall back.

As such, they merit our scholarly attention and also our intelligent solidarity.

A COMMENTARY: THE CASE OF MODERN TURKEY

Ervand Abrahamian

I would like to begin by congratulating Jean Piel for a fascinating and highly comprehensive study. Since I fully agreed with much of his presentation on the relationship between state and society in Western history, I will direct my comments to those aspects with which I disagreed, that is the last section discussing the future role of the state in transforming non-Western societies. In this section Jean Piel has tended to discard his Marxist realism of seeing the state as an organization within the framework of social conflicts. Instead he has adopted — like many Western social scientists, especially American political scientists — a Hegelian perspective of idealizing the state as standing above society and thus capable of "modernizing", "transforming", and "revolutionizing" non-Western societies. He has consequently concluded with what I feel is an over-optimistic prediction of possible transformations in the Third World. He would have reached a less optimistic conclusion if he had treated the non-Western state with the same Marxist methodology he had treated the Western states — as an organization sought after by different forces within society.

In stating that the Marxist approach is useful for analyzing the relaticnship between state and society, I am not claiming that the future developments in the Third World will duplicate exactly the past experiences of the West. The Third World and the West have three undeniable differences. First, imperialism has incorporated many former colonies into its economic, social, and political orbits. Consequently, the capitalist bourgeoisie, which played a vital role in such European transformations as the French Revolution, is now in the Third World an extension of the conservative imperial interest of the West. Second, class cleavages in the Third World are often complicated by communal ties of tribe, language, ethnicity, region, and religion. These communal ties do not eradicate class consciousness — as many Western social scientists would claim — but merely complicate the politics of social conflict. Third, in the non-Western world the salaried intelligentsia, as opposed to the capitalist bourgeoisie, is playing a much more independent and therefore significant role than it ever did in the West. In many new states the intelligentsia has already gained power. In others it is struggling to gain power — often against the traditional landed class. Thus the crucial question is: Will the intelligentsia use state power to carry through major transformations of society benefiting the masses? Or will it only initiate limited reforms which do not fundamentally change society, but do strengthen the middle classes? The experiences of countries where the intelligentsia has seized power lead one to the pessimistic conclusion that all we can expect are limited reforms, not fundamental transformations.

This conclusion can be illustrated by the case of modern Turkey. The intelligentsia, headed by Mustafa Kemal — later famous as Ataturk — entered the political arena at the end of World War I appearing to be a dynamic revolutionary class. It led the Anatolian peasantry in a successful guerrilla war of national liberation against the imperial powers, and created out of the ruins of the Ottoman Empire the new state of modern Turkey. It replaced the sultanate with a republic, abolished the caliphate, organized a Republican Party, and, creating a one-party state, carried through a series of reforms. Economic capitulations to European interests, some of which originated as far back as the sixteenth century, were abolished. Friendly relations were instead established with the Soviet Union: Turkey was one of the first to sign a treaty of friendship with the Soviet Union. The capital was moved away from Istanbul, on the doorstep of the West, to Anatolia in the heartland of Turkey. Militant secularism attacked the traditional clergy: Koranic schools were replaced by government schools, religious courts by state courts, the Arabic script with the Latin script; religion was eliminated from the educational system, from the mass media, and formally from the new constitution; and members of the clergy found it almost impossible to work in state institutions, join the Republican Party, or enter the National Assembly. A series of Five Year Plans, moreover, initiated some economic and social reforms. The state discouraged foreign capital with high tariffs and taxes, but, at the same time, encouraged internal development with government investments for transport, education, and national industries, including a steel mill built with the help of the Soviet Union.

These developments, however, constituted impressive reforms, but not a fundamental revolution. Secularism forced the clergy out of politics: it did not bring the masses into political participation. Five Year Plans gave many benefits for the middle classes, but almost none for the working and peasant classes. Most of the expenditures went into the military establishment, consumer industries, urban housing, municipal roads, government offices, and into higher education — in short, into the middle-income strata located in the towns. And most of the revenue for these projects was extracted from the urban and rural masses through consumer taxes, control of the agricultural market, long work hours, low wages, a lowering of the standard of living, and, during World War II, through unpaid forced labor. The reforms in modern Turkey, therefore, were paid for by the masses, but they came from the intelligentsia, were carried out by them and were designed for the benefit of them.

Many of the reforms, moreover, were undermined after Ataturk's death. In order to attract foreign capital, government restrictions on external trade were removed, state intervention in the economy was supplanted by a policy of laissez-faire, and neutralism was abandoned for the sake of a staunch pro-Western alliance. And in order to win over the commercial bourgeoisie within the country, secularism was toned down, state enterprises were de-nationalized, and the government formally committed itself to the ideology of economic development through private enterprise. The reforming, and seemingly revolutionary Turkey of the 1920s. was now succeeded by the conservative Turkey of the 1950s.

If we use the Turkish experience to judge the potentiality of the intelligentsia in other parts of the world, we have to reach a pessimistic conclusion — at least for the possibilities of revolution in the near-future. In some countries, the intelligentsia may use the state in order to initiate reforms. In other countries, it may use the means of coercion in order to conserve the *status quo*. But it is unlikely to mobilize any state in order to carry through a fundamental transformation of society — a transformation which would inevitably destroy its own elite position.

However, I would like to point to some rays of optimistic light in the distant future. The intelligentsia, in implementing reforms, unwittingly and gradually prepares the way for a possible revolution. Industrialization, with or without the help of the multi-national corporations, brings into existence an urban working class — a class that is new, always highly exploited, invariably discontented, and often revolutionary. Changes in the countryside, such as limited land reform, extension of the means of communication, a rise in literacy, and an increase in population, intensifies class differences in the villages — class differences which had been overshadowed by traditional ties in the past. And "modernization" of the military and bureaucracy results in an expansion of the educational facilities, which, in turn, results in an expansion in the ranks of a new generation of the intelligentsia — a generation which is not satisfied with the limited aspirations of the previous one. When the state is no longer the monopoly of a particular class, I may be able to share Jean Piel's optimism, and see the state as the vanguard of revolution. But until that time I will stress the point that, in order to have a revolutionary state, one must first have a viable revolutionary class.

WORLD INEQUALITY:
trans-national movements

INTERNATIONAL WORKERS' MOVEMENT

Albert-Paul Lentin

THE world in 1974 is characterized by an extensive international division of labour. There is a core, mainly dominated by the international capitalist system, and a periphery. I think we can compare this world to the two poles of a compass: wealth breeds wealth and poverty. The core develops and the periphery, as a whole, underdevelops. Within the peripheral sector of the compass, there is if you will another compass. There one finds development, or rather growth, some poles which develop, but which in the larger compass are centres of underdevelopment. In this situation the working classes are in an ambiguous position. In the developed world, the workers are exploited by the dominating capitalist system, which reaps the bulk of the profits. However, these working classes receive some crumbs, because of the pillage of the Third World, they also obtain a share of this global pillage. Hence the ambiguity of their position. And in the underdeveloped countries, the working classes are also exploited by the dominant neo-colonial system. However, they enjoy a privileged position when compared to the peasants and the urban unemployed. Indeed, the mere fact of having a job, a secure job, when the number of unemployed is so large, places them in an ambiguous position.

It is within this context that one must consider international workers' movements. I shall concentrate on the industrial capitalist world since others are analyzing the situation in the Third World. Indeed, if one is to study inequalities in international relations, we have to look at what is going on in the core of the capitalist world, because it too is plagued with inequalities. Let me draw a short historical sketch, using the framework given by Mr. Wolff, i.e., an early phase of capitalism in the era of British hegemony (1848-1948), then a second phase in the aftermath of World War II, the era of American hegemony, and finally, the latest phase which I would call the phase of capitalist *latent crisis*, that of the multinationals. In the classical phase of capitalism, workers' exploitation was at its peak and the phase was characterized by violent conflicts, the lines of which have not changed since. Conflicts were concerned with wages, the length of the working day (the problem of overtime, paid leave, etc.), working conditions, sanitation, workmen's compensation, job security against unemployment, and finally, the problem of professional training and retraining. These conflicts were so intense that quite spontaneously the idea emerged that those who waged them throughout the capitalist system had common goals which transcended patriotism, the national loyalties of the past. This period represented, I think, the apogee of proletarian internationalism, the theme expressed in the Communist Manifesto in the formula, the proletariat had no homeland. Proletarian internationalism was also found in the trade unions. Trade union leaders of different countries rapidly established contacts in an effort to develop common strategies. In the political sphere, there was the First and then the Second International. Workers' inspirations expressed an increasingly internationalist ethics in their struggle against the inequalities prevailing within the capitalist system. In the periphery of the time, there were struggles for the emancipation of colonial peoples. However, in those days it was believed that the working classes of industrialized countries, by coming to power in advanced countries, would liberate the workers of the world. This view was marked by a large degree of egocentrism, which accounts for many of the contradictions to be found in the First and the Second International. This also occurred at the birth of the Communist International, the non-Europocentric theses of Sultan Galier being rejected at the very beginning of the Bolshevik Revolution.

In the period between the World Wars things changed, because of a crucial development during the First World War. This War, in my opinion, marked the end of proletarian internationalism. Why? Because two tendencies had emerged in the international workers' movement: one very radical, expressing the belief that wars were unavoidable, since they represented the ultimate form of internal capitalist struggle. The competition for markets inevitably tended to wars between the great capitalist powers. At the same time, they thought that a general strike of all workers on both sides would prevent war from taking place. There was also the moderate viewpoint, which was that the same result could be achieved simply through pressure on governments. This was more or less the view characterizing the majority of French socialists led by Jaurès. In fact, both attempts failed. Nationalism was more powerful a force and, both in France and in Germany, socialists joined the "sacred union." Albert Thomas and Guesde entered the War cabinet in France as early as October 1914, and in Germany, there were deals with Chancellor Bethmann-Hollweg. In both cases, the more radical socialists who refused to join the war-time sacred union were in the minority. This caused a basic split.

From 1918 to 1945, nationalism was on the rise, and still is today. This is, I believe, a basic reality. The core of the world-system experienced an extension of nationalist sentiment, precisely because the masses had become more politicized, and thus, superficially, at least, the game was no longer limited to the political classes. Mass media developed. Quite easily, involvement of the masses took on the form of allegiance to charismatic ideas. The whole process was truly superficial, and based on only the most elementary nationalist sentiments. In the periphery, there was the struggle for independence of the movements of national liberation led by nationalist petty bourgeoisies manufactured by the system, who assumed the leadership of these movements. As an initial step they aimed at political decolonization, i.e. national sovereignty, entrance into the United Nations, a national flag, etc. This movement has been extremely powerful and successful, as during the years 1955-1960, this movement won its objectives, in the first wave of political decolonization.

The socialist camp also experienced a strong nationalist current, initiated by the appearance of the Soviet Union on the international scene, this Soviet Union which gained so much influence as a result of the Second World War. It created a protective ring of allied European states around it, while the movement occurred that would lead to the victory of the Chinese Revolution in 1949 and ten years later, in Cuba. Why? I believe that within the socialist camp we saw the deviations first from Leninism to Stalinism, then the thesis of revolution in one country. That is to say, the USSR became the fundamental centre of the revolutionary movement; the dissolution of the Comintern in 1943 only underlined an evolution whereby the theory of polycentric internationalism which had characterized the early days of Lenin was replaced by the dogma of Soviet leadership in anything related to the revolutionary movement. Then came the internal crises of Stalinism at the ideological level. Such were the constraints, contradictions and cleavages, that the only ideology that remained was that of Great Russian nationalism which inspired Soviet resistance to Nazi advances in 1939-45.

We thus find nationalism everywhere. This period was marked by a general decline in workers' and proletarian internationalism. At the political level, the phase is characterized by the deep split between social democracy and international communism. The split came as early as 1920 and, for quite a long period of time, the antagonism between the two remained virulent. Its effects spilled over to the trade-union movements. After World War II, there was founded, on the one hand, the ICFTU, International Confederation of Free Trade Unions (and, to a lesser extent, the International Federation of Christian Trade Unions) which was highly influenced by American workers' movements both in its strong concept of sectarial bread-and-butter trade-unionism and in its foreign policy views, very anti-Soviet and anti-communist. On the other hand there was the World Federation of Trade Unions (WFTU) which included a new form of trade-unionism: state trade-unionism. That is, in Communist countries, the political and union bureaucracies overlapped, and in accordance with the theory of functioning as a transmission belt, the unions existed to carry out the decisions arrived at within the party structures, among the mass of the workers. Such unions thus had essentially a managerial function. They existed to take care of problems of housing, and of the social and cultural problems of the enterprises. They were also supposed to assist in increasing production, the prime goal of these countries, especially since they wished to catch up with the capitalist world. Therefore the purely political role as well as the role of confronting the managers of the enterprises was quite weak. There were crises at times. While we shall not go into these, it does underline the fact that there are some highly different worlds of the workers, and that between them, solidarity was very relative.

As far as the periphery is concerned, solidarities were also quite relative, as it was still a period of rebellion, and nationalist elements, including the workers, were against the paternalism and the Europo-centric attitude of the workers' movement of the previous phase. The relationships were thus complicated. Even when these peripheral movements joined world groupings of trade-unions, either for tactical reasons the ICFTU, or for other reasons the WFTU, they did so for opportunistic reasons and the motives and objectives were quite different from those of these world structures.

I now come to the second era, that of American hegemony, which brings us up to the 1960's. Some brief points will clarify the state of the worker internationalism at the time. First, following the first industrial revolution of coal and steel, a second revolution occurred, that of petroleum, synthetic fibres, plastics, the atom, with the rise of a new proletariat of highly qualified labour. Within the working classes, important differentiation occurs. Secondly, in the diplomatic arena, the world becomes bipolarized between the superpowers, the U.S. and the USSR. Measures which in the short run were designed to revive capitalist economies badly damaged by World War II, gave new life to the potentially staunchest rivals of American capitalism. The capitalists of the 19th century were on the decline, as the taking over of France's role in Indochina by the end of Britain's and France's leading roles, as the U.S. and the USSR both stepped in to become the privileged partners of the area.

From 1955-60 on, the balance of terror led to peaceful coexistence and, at a larger stage, to peaceful cooperation. This goes beyond a mere nuclear coexistence, into a close industrial cooperation. This is the period in which we are presently living. The U.S. is investing technology and offering long term loans to the Soviet Union. It is a very important moment as one may be seeing the process of convergence between the capitalist system and the socialist one, at least, in its Soviet version. The same might happen with the Chinese, given the American-Chinese agreements. The Chinese at least are limiting relations with the capitalist system to the level of trade. They do not contemplate formulas such as the technological investment taking place in the Soviet Union and which is evidenced by the opening of a huge Chase Manhattan Bank building on Moscow's Karl Marx Square. This is about the best example one can get. It means that there is a link-up between the two systems at the world level.

All these events create problems for the working class. For example, the trade-unions of Eastern Europe have their ideology. It is worker solidarity with West-European workers against the producers of capitalist countries, especially if these latter belong to the same world confederation, as is the case for France and Italy. However, at the same time, to further their country's growth, East European governments have to rely on the credit facilities and the technology of the large capitalist firms as can be seen from the recent political developments between East and West. For these trade unions, there are clearly a host of contradictions to resolve. As far as the periphery is concerned, the pillage of the Third World's resources increases as neo-colonialism expands, brushing aside its outmoded aspects — direct domination, military domination — and pursuing single-mindedly the goal of maximizing economic returns. The split between workers from developed countries and workers from the under-developed ones cannot but widen, even if trade-unions follow the path of Stalinist bureaucratization. That is, to the degree that technocratic bourgeoisies take control in most Third World countries while maintaining their links with former metropoles, they in fact use a single-party system without adopting its ideology. But the ideology was originally revolutionary and socialist. They adopt only the methods and govern through single-party systems. However they strive to domesticate as rapidly as possible the existing trade-unions. In fact, most Third World countries' unions are state trade-unions which, in effect, renders worker protest difficult. Either the workers utilize the state trade-unions and they are limited by the ruling classes, or they reject these unions, become marginalized and are subject to repression. With respect to the industrial capitalist world, as far as international workers' movements are concerned, we have reached the ultimate of what I would call "reformist solidarity." That is, everywhere it is thought that the system is acceptable, that development should proceed, and that the main problem involved is improving the management of these systems which would then enable the working classes to reap the most advantages from the capitalist system. Concessions should be wrested from the employers (not unimportant ones), but without calling into question the system itself. This is what I would term the ICFTU line of negotiating collective agreements. It implies a definition of the social contract to be obtained. There may be some long strikes (the American style), involving much effort and large outlays of funds, but once the objective is reached, the matter is closed. The system remains and no question is raised anymore about the ultimate goals of the system.

If there are no major confrontations coming from the other side, it is because both sides agree that the USSR, on the one hand, and the U.S., on the other, each have their spheres of influence, and that confrontation shall only occur in a few intermediate areas. Thus, there is no longer a Communist-inspired revolutionary thrust. There has been a considerable lag in Cold War ideology which still talks about Communist subversion, when the Communist parties have already decided that what they want is improved management of capitalism and not radical upheaval which would upset the world's equilibrium. This was clearly the case with France in the 1966-70 period. From the notion of violent revolution, Communist leaders have moved to the idea of the legal road to socialism via a parliamentary majority. Through progressive changes, power will be obtained peacefully, non-violently, and then very slowly the State apparatus will be altered. In recent years, this trend has been strengthened and nowadays one may see attempts to bring the WFTU and the ICFTU together. Despite their former extreme antagonism, they are now at the stage of reaching a modus vivendi on common problems they face in the International Labour Organization and elsewhere. Backward elements in the U.S. have protested, to be sure. The AFL-CIO takes these developments badly, and thus has created internal problems for the American trade-union movement.

I now come to my third era, that of today, the one I see as characterized by latent crisis, and the rise of the multinationals. Why latent crisis? I believe we have reached the stage where the contradictions between the periphery and the core have grown to such proportions that it now is provoking a crisis within the core. Let me be more specific. For quite a long period of time, in comparison with the U.S., all countries were underdeveloped. Because the U.S. was so technologically advanced, investment outside of the U.S. appeared more profitable than investing inside the U.S. There was a strong outbound movement of capital from the U.S. across the world, particularly into the underdeveloped countries, a movement whereby capital reaped rewards elsewhere, then to the U.S., then went outward again, renewing this cycle. This flow created huge balance of payments and trade deficits for the U.S. as well as an inflationary spiral which finally erupted into a full-fledged monetary crisis. It finally led to the devaluation of the dollar and, even more important, to the abandonment of the sacred rules arrived at during the Bretton Woods negotiations. Now we are in a crisis because everyone agrees the International Monetary Fund must be reformed but disagrees on how to do so. Furthermore, the peripheral countries are demanding greater participation in running the IMF. We thus are at a stage of combined stagnation and inflation, and the general crisis is aggravated by the contradiction between the varying centers of capitalism and imperialism. German capitalism is about to take the leadership of European capitalism. Combined with Japanese capitalism they are both in a position effectively to challenge American capitalism, while French and British capitalism maintain strong positions especially in their traditional areas of influence, such as the Mediterranean.

Thus we have a latent crisis — latent because it in no way resembles the crisis of 1929. It is not a battle to gain markets, an issue of over-production. It is a crisis of internal relationships, which means that although capitalism is capable of maintaining itself, even to grow and expand, its internal mechanisms are greatly disturbed. Hence the constant oscillations of inflationary phenomena and instability of the superstructure, a value "super-crisis."

At the same time as this fundamental crisis, essential ideological values are being very seriously questioned within the capitalist world, first in the United States and, progressively, in Europe. Thus capitalism may recover but it has been shaken. However, nowadays, its continued expansion depends more and more on the multinationals. Nonetheless, the national frame is by no means eliminated from the picture. Indeed, it still is very important. First, because multinational companies ultimately have a home base for banking and financial decisions. In fact, this fact attests to the fundamental domination of industrial capital by financial capital. If one looks around, one can readily see that the power behind the multinationals are the main banks. The three German giants are the Dresdener Bank, the Deutsche Bank and the Commerz Bank. Thus, multinational corporations have a national imprint. Furthermore, multinational corporations do not control all the levers of action. This is a very important aspect of a capitalist world. While they may have their private intelligence services, they have no armies, no forces that can intervene for them, and thus in the political arena, they have to rely on the apparatus of the state. ITT may very well have thought that land expropriation in Chile was scandalous and that Allende's regime ought to be overthrown, but when they decided to do it, they had to rely on the CIA, to call in forces belonging to the American state. Thus, while multinational corporations do raise new problems, they are definitely linked to state capitalism.

These enterprises tend to monopolize key production sectors of the capitalist world. They have long done so in the petroleum industry. All international petroleum companies except the Anglo-Dutch Royal Dutch Shell are U.S.-based. They are about to control the nuclear energy field. In fact, these same U.S.-based petroleum companies are presently investing huge amounts in atomic research and ten years from now they will control that field. They are also in the process of completely dominating the international capitalist market of computer technology, including space computer technology, as well as the pure chemicals industry and affiliated branches such as pharmaceuticals, rubber, glass, paper, etc. There are now vast sectors of the world production in the hands of the multinationals. When these various companies join to share in resource development, the level of production they are able to achieve is enormous. More than 50% of capitalist production is already being carried on by the multinationals. Within five years this percentage will have risen to 60 or 70% and by 1980-85, it will have reached 85%. Because at the same time they cooperate with each other in joint capitalist interests, they will have multiple activities or "multi-activities." That is, while a multinational, in general, controls a primary production sector (petroleum, chemicals, automobile), it also conducts, in the interests of profit, a host of secondary activities which may include hotel chains, television, tourism, etc. There is thus an increasing concentration of production.

What happens then to the labour world faced with this re-shaped capitalist system. At the level of what I have called reformist solidarity there is a modest initial awareness of the multinationals and beginning consciousness of their meaning. Some efforts are being made to adapt to this reality, mainly within the ICFTU, precisely because it is its members who are directly under the control of the multinationals. However, when one considers things as they presently stand one has to acknowledge the advanced stage of capitalist cosmopolitanism compared to the relative backwardness of workers and trade-union internationalism. Multinational corporations have a series of trumps in their hands in relation to the world of the workers and the class struggle. First of all, multinationals have their legal and administrative headquarters around the world in fiscal paradises, Puerto Rico, Belgium, etc. Thus they are out of direct contact with the workers. Second, they wield such political influence that they can force governments to favour them through legislative measures despite the fragile barriers which states have tried to erect, most often as token gestures, such as the U.S. anti-trust laws, Bonn's Kartelamt and even the EEC's far-reaching measures. Third, they can invest in research and technology projects in external institutions which are huge, and autonomous, scientific entities. These are, to a great extent, free from taxation. Their means are such that in addition to technological invention, they can also accelerate production processes. Technological unemployment results, as technological revolutions leave old cadres behind. Multinationals can also transfer production from one place to another. When there is a strike in one country, production is transferred and/or expanded in another country where the multinational has a production unit. Worker's solidarity in these cases can only manifest itself through supportive action. The only solution for workers would, in effect, be transnational strikes and/or other measures.

To conclude I wish to indicate that in addition to this renewed workers' international solidarity of the reformist variety, there is also a renewed revolutionary workers solidarity which rejects the notion of capitalist reform in favour of the downfall of capitalism. Why? Simply because there are changes, deep changes in working class attitudes. Capitalist expansion has integrated workers aristocracies, but has left some important groups of producers marginal: women who increasingly want to work, youth, and especially the migratory workers. This is where the dialectics of periphery and core comes back in. While in the initial phase capitalism's main concern was to acquire the Third World's primary resources, now there is a strong tendency to bring cheap manpower from the periphery into developed countries. Colonialism has moved from an external to an internal pattern. France has 3.5 million foreign workers, Germany has workers from Europe's periphery, i.e. Greece, Turkey, Portugal, etc. There is a new labour class, not only a lumpenproletariat, of unskilled labourers. Tensions, while unorganized, are spreading. Revolutionary ideology and praxis are revived, occasionally in an infantile form. For everything must be discovered again, re-invented. It is a moment of sectarianism, infantilism, ideological frenzies. However, it is also a period of daring, in which something is happening. There are phenomena which are new for us but also very important and appear to signal the resurgence of revolutionary solidarity within international workers' movements.

THE MOVEMENT OF ARAB UNITY

Mohamed Harbi

DURING the last two decades three States have constantly advocated Arab unity, Syria, Iraq, and Egypt, as have several pan-Arab movements — Nasserism, the Baath, the Arab National Movement. These have obtained support from various social strata: workers, peasants, intellectuals. They have mobilized the hopes and acts of political forces and peoples which were fighting to gain or regain their independence. Therefore, and notwithstanding the doubts and questions the enterprise may raise, one cannot consider it as the expression of a collective fantasy but rather as a fundamental dimension of Arab social dynamics. Any serious approach to this phenomenon must avoid lyrical illusions and rely on hard data and their significance. In order to do that, we must analyze the process of capitalist penetration and elucidate some of the fundamental changes which it has brought to the structure of the Arab world.

From the 19th century on, the Arab world was progressively integrated into the world capitalist market. In this process, the Arab West preceded the Arab East. The capitalist mode of production was restricted to specific sectors. Along with the pillage of raw materials came the invasion of finished products. New conditions of life and work emerged. Old social structures disintegrated without, however, establishing a social framework similar to that of industrial societies. Evolution towards a fully capitalist structure did not occur. The Arab world reached modernity without its accompanying material foundations. Paraphrasing Marx on capitalist development in

Germany, I would say that the Arab world is afflicted by the development of capitalist production and by its nondevelopment. In addition to the evils of today, it suffers from a long series of hereditary evils resulting from the continued survival of antiquated modes of production and the unbalanced political and social consequences such survival creates. It not only suffers because of the living, but because of the dead.

Dependency and under-development of productive forces account for specific characteristics in the socio-economic formations. Social cleavages do not take the same form they do in industrial societies. In nearly all these countries, whose development furthermore is extremely unequal, the low level of industrialization results in having the proletariat nowhere in the majority. It exists within a universe where the petty bourgeoisie, the peasants and the unemployed predominate. The persistence of ideologies inherited from the past, most particularly the influence of the Moslem religion, keeps the social structure and politics from corresponding. It is therefore pointless to try to link the attitudes of oppressed classes exclusively to their economic situation. Doing so would be tantamount to minimizing the role of history and its presence in contemporary consciousness.

Today, most of the Arab world is organized in nation-states. With the independence of South Yemen and the Federation of Arab Emirates, the classical form of colonialism has disappeared in this region. What deserves to be underlined is that the political struggle matured differently in each country. In the course of this struggle, the slogan of unity took shape, and in the process became a rallying-point.

From an ethical and religious point of view, the geographic area subject to Arabo-Islamic conquest is not homogeneous. Some examples may illustrate this point.

In Iraq and in the Sudan, the Kurdish and Anya-Anya minorities have raised the issue of self-determination. In Algeria and Morocco, Berber particularism is ignored but exists nonetheless.

More importantly, the economies of Arab countries are more directed towards the industrialized countries than they are linked to each other. Intra-Arab trade is limited. Pan-Arab projects and regional unions attempts (Maghreb and Machrek) have not induced major reorientations. The increasing number of commercial agreements cannot hide the stiff competition prevailing between Arab countries. For example, Algeria, Tunisia and Morocco each built metallurgy complexes despite their being perfectly aware that, at some stage, they will face a market problem.

Political science literature divides the Arab countries into two groups: conservatives and progressives. This classification is rather ambiguous, particularly nowadays as it doesn't do justice to real tendencies in each country and conceals the limits of anti-imperialistic conceptions within the Arab petty bourgeoisie as well as the class character of the states. In fact, both conservative and progressive Arab states are equally involved in a capitalist path of development.

The progressives seek to take advantage of conflicts of interest between the great powers, especially the U.S. and the USSR, in order to solve their development problems.

The conservatives pledge allegiance to the West and say they follow the banner of liberalism even if the State carries the major burden of economic life. Foreign policy and the nationalization of activities are not sufficient as criteria to differentiate one regime from another. At most, they can provide information on the social origin of the leadership, about their political concepts and their ideology.

The use of modern culture as a weapon for national and social liberation involves a series of contradictions. To the problem of an ancient culture made obsolete by the integration of its living elements and the rejection of its outmoded elements, Arab bourgeois and petty-bourgeois have substituted a false dilemma: Westernization vs. traditionalism. The aim is clearly political. They seek to preserve and channel those values which favor national unity, and close the door to any class struggle.

From the general characteristics of the Arab world one can deduce that no transnational movement can tie its existence to a rigid ethical or religious concept without risking cutting itself off from whole communities. In fact the three movements that have dominated the political life of the Arab world in the recent past, i.e.: Nasserism, the Baath, and the Arab nationalists, consider the Islamic legacy as an integral part of their historical patrimony, but, at the same time, none subordinates its political perspectives to religion.

No one can deny that the appearance of nationalist concepts in dominated countries is the belated popular answer to the situation created by imperialism. The transnational idea of Arab unity is a similar reaction. It emerged in a geographically well defined area: Arab Asia. Why precisely there? History provides the key: Syria has been the cradle of Arab nationalism. Its territory, as defined in the period following World War II, was only one part of a larger ensemble which included Palestine and Lebanon. The breakdown of this unit into three distinct entities was decided jointly by France and Great Britain. The majority of the population, which had expected the creation of a unitary Arab state, greeted the decision as an unacceptable challenge, the more so since in Palestine, under British mandate, a Jewish state was allowed to grow up at the expense of the Arab inhabitants. Right from the start, the liberation of Palestine became a fundamental premise of Arab unitary ideology. The nationalist claims of "small Syria" thus became a transnational protest against balkanization.

In the aftermath of World War I, the movement for Arab unity acquired some support among the Egyptian ruling classes. The bourgeoisie of this country came to realize that its own political and economic growth was tied to the Arab geographic zone. In that sense Gamal Abd-el-Nasser is the true successor of Talaat Harb, founder of the MISR group and bank, and of the Wefdist leader, Makram Ebeid, who, despite the isolationist tendencies of large sectors within Egyptian public opinion, was to proclaim, in 1935, that Egypt belonged to the Arab world.

For a long time, the movement for Arab unity remained purely a phenomenon of the Arab east. In the Maghreb, it was overshadowed by cultural Arabism and Islamism. There was one exception however, Libya. In 1937, the Tripolitan leader Suleyman El Barouni initiated a vigorous polemic with Emir Chakib Arslan who, during the first congress on Arab unity (Syria, 12 March 1973) excluded the Maghreb from any formal union with Arab countries, and accused him of an unavowed concession to French colonialism.

In Algeria, Ben Badis agreed with Chakib Arslan. What the Maghrebians asked from the Eastern Arabs was for some help in their struggle for national independence. From thereon, the Maghreb countries always approached the search for unity from a very particular perspective and set of problems.

In 1960 Colonel Boumédienne asserted the primacy of Algerian nationalism over any other path. In a message to the Provisional Government of the Algerian Republic, he requested the mobilization of every student "to detract them from the influence of Nasserism, Baathism and Marxism." Those who, like Ben Bella, or Salah Ben Youssef, have attempted to integrate their national strategy within the framework of a strategy for the unity of Arab peoples have always represented a minority even if, among the masses, there is a feeling of shared destiny with the Eastern Arabs.

Thus, in the face of the history and the realities of the Arab world, the movement for unity lost the imminence given it by the ideologues of Arab nationalism. It showed itself to be before all the product of the economic and political situation of the Arab East at the beginning of the century and not merely the expression of some ancient mysticism.

The variety of paths leading to unity readily explains the lack of homogeneity and the presence of cleavages which characterizes Arab nationalist attitudes and approaches.

Arab nationalism and the organizations which acted as its spokesmen have played a major role in the development of anti-imperialist struggles. For the oppressed Arab peoples, solidarity is a must. It grew out of an increasing national consciousness and the simple need to gather forces to fight the enemy. It rests upon a feeling of common history, on geographical contiguity and on linguistic similarity. In all Arab countries political life emerged under conditions of foreign domination. Arabism capitalized on cries for dignity and freedom. It incarnated hope in times of distress. It cannot therefore be reduced to a mere feudal or bourgeois conception of the world. It is in the name of Arabism that feudal lords rebelled against the Ottoman Empire and, later, against the British. But it is also in the name of Arabism that the feudal society was destroyed by the formerly subservient classes, and this for a precise reason: the lords could no longer meet the needs of the Arab masses.

Throughout the Arab world, the national movement vanquished colonialism in its classical form. But it has failed to develop adequate solutions to over-come under-development and eliminate Zionism and imperialism. The feudal strata, the bourgeoisie, and the petty-bourgeoisie have followed each other in the social arena. Each deserves a quota of blame. At the beginning of the British mandate,

Arab resistance in Palestine was dominated by feudal lords and opportunists. The same strata, which the Turks had formerly used to control the masses, placed themselves at the service of the British and encouraged Zionist colonization by selling land to the highest bidder. Every spontaneous popular uprising has found itself confronted by nationalism and its supporters: the national exploiters.

The armed insurrection of 1936-39 and the six-month general strike also originated from initially spontaneous movements which the leaders joined in order to bring them under control. The defeat of the Arab armies in 1948 against the Zionist state announced the end of feudal and bourgeois dynasties, and the rise of a new leadership drawn from the army.

The "petty-bourgeoisie" appears on the scene, first in Egypt, where a group of officers brought down the corrupt monarchy of King Farouk.

As in the previous era this class was confronted with the Palestine question as well as with the problems of national and social liberation. Its first major initiative was the nationalization of the Suez Canal which led to the tripartite aggression of 1956. Throughout the Arab world, masses longing for dignity, freedom and well-being, deprived of everything, discovered Nasser, the man who had dared to oppose imperialism. Power now fell into the hands of the petty-bourgeoisie which, by a social transformation, had now a State bureaucracy. Its leader and representative, Nasser, then sought to gather all Arab peoples around Egypt. The existence of Israel favoured this concept but the new ruling class had its own interests, its separate objectives. The union with Syria within the United Arab Republic fell apart. The tendency of the Egyptian state to achieve hegemony ran counter to the particularisms of Syrian interest groups. Arab nationalism had thus demonstrated its limits and the Arab petty-bourgeoisie the lack of depth of its convictions.

The defeat of Arab armies against Israel in 1967 was the defeat of classes which pretended to change everything even when no change came from within, not their aspiration, nor their suspicion of the masses, nor their natural tendency to compromise with imperialism. Nasser had symbolized a longing for unity at the level of the masses, particularly within oppressed classes which lacked any objective social power and which, given their inability to help themselves, sought external help from the "top." However, Nasser remained the representative of the strata which exploited the masses. The Israeli challenge would tarnish his credibility and his death would precipitate the crisis of the Arab nationalist movement. None of the other movements for unity — whether Baath, or the Arab nationalists — have the popular support which Nasser enjoyed. None was capable of bringing about significant change. Their promises proved to be illusory because they incarnated the goals of the middle class. When pushed to the outer limits, they always fell back on conjectural explanations. Marx's analysis of the democratic petty-bourgeoisie in France is readily applicable: "The democrat comes out of the most disgraceful defeat just as immaculate as he went into it innocent, with the newly-won conviction that he is bound to conquer, not that he himself and his party have to give up the old standpoint, but, on the contrary, that conditions have to ripen in his direction." (K. Marx, The 18th Brumaire of Louis Bonaparte).

Some think that Kadhafi is a possible leader for Arab nationalism. Was it not he that managed to get the Tunisian bourgeoisie to leave its national ghetto? It may be that history, in order to announce a failure — in this case, that of Bourguibism seeking capital to remedy an ever-deepening social crisis — chooses a messenger who makes himself available. But, this messenger has to be able to play the role. Kadhafi cannot. His religious proselytism drags the Arab world back into its distant past. Anyway, he doesn't possess the means required to implement his policy. He may have an occasional success, improve his position. But he cannot succeed in getting himself accepted as the leader of the Arab petty-bourgeoisie.

For quite some time, after the defeat of June 1967, the Palestinian resistance constituted a possible rallying-point of the Arab world. However, the absence of a clear analysis of the Palestinian national question and the incapacity on the part of Palestinians to understand that the real contradiction is neither Zionism vs. resistance nor Arab reaction vs. resistance but imperialism vs. dominated classes. This has dragged them into the same mistakes which had caused their earlier failures, and pushed them back into the arms of the very states that embrace them in order to snuff them out.

The experience of the PDFLP is illuminating in that respect. This organization recruited Arab fighters by the hundreds from all countries. But its desire to have diplomatic relations with the vari-

ous Arab states soon forced it to ask non-Palestinian Arabs to re-
nounce the idea of an Arab revolution in favour of an emphasis on
Palestine. And thus it alienated many supporters.

The hegemony of Arab nationalism over the movement for
Arab unity is drawing to its end. It has had tangible, positive results.
It has accustomed people to conceiving of action outside of and
beyond existing frontiers. National liberation struggles have been
waged in its name. However, none of these struggles has led to the
definitive eradication of imperialist influence. Direct domination has
disappeared in Arab countries, but the memory of old conflicts remains very much present at the ideological level. The disappearance
of colonialism clarifies the issue. It has removed inherited obstacles
from the battlefield where the exploiters and the exploited shall now
confront each other. This accounts for why the so-called progressive
Arab countries place such importance in their ideology on the denunciation of the remnants of colonialism, of neo-colonialism and of
imperialism. This denunciation of an external enemy serves to hide
the internal exploitation. The action of imperialism has now become
indirect, and can only operate via the complicity of intermediaries it
finds within each country.

The Arab ruling classes, whatever their social origins, are incapable of carrying out fully their objectives. History is indeed a
cruel goddess. No mask can long prevent its judgement. These leaders, while they wish to terminate Israel's hegemony in this area,
want to do so without ending their own hegemony over the worker
and peasant masses.

All the states are linked either to the world imperialist
economy or to the USSR, or sometimes to both. Whatever they may
want, this economic dependence makes them pawns of the battle for
influence between the U.S.A. and the USSR. Their destiny is therefore one of compromise and of giving in. Imperialism perpetuates itself because of the contradictions it sustains. Palestinians and Is-
realis can live side by side, but only without Zionism and without
Arab nationalism which justify one another and create a perpetual
impasse.

The bourgeoisie and the petty-bourgeoisie are incapable of
achieving Arab unity, either under the Prussian model or through
some federal or confederal arrangement. Their model cannot but be
that of a League of States, i.e. a form which carries no obligation.

They are also incapable of allowing the self-assertion of minorities and particularisms. And without that, all the speeches about harmony between the ethnic groups located in the Middle-East are nothing but deceit.

Any union which would take into account the interests of all classes could only reproduce the competition prevailing among the Arab ruling classes and between them and their imperialist masters.

The Arab geographic and socio-cultural world constitutes a legacy favourable to the maturation of a consciousness oriented towards radical change. Each time one country enters in struggle, it radicalizes the social and political aspirations throughout the Arab zone and becomes a factor in the internal policy of each state. We must therefore look at the real conditions under which the struggles are fought. To conceive, as the Communist parties do, of the class struggle as the composite of various struggles, carried on separately in individual countries, is to accept a strategy which runs counter to interests of Arab workers. Indeed, it exposes them to serious dangers. Within a limited arena, the advantage is mainly with the powers that be. One might even say that the unity of the governments is way ahead of the unity of revolutionary forces. Sadat and Kadhafi intervened to save Numeiry and to block any possibility of revolution in the Sudan, as has Ibn Saud's constant action against South Yemen, via the northern tribes. This clearly demonstrates that to refuse the framework of a pan-Arab struggle will only hurt the masses.

Under the present conditions, no Arab country alone can achieve national development, following the path of the European countries. Algeria and Egypt are neither China nor the USSR. The existing potential of the Arab world, the limits of the present industrialization process, should induce us to give short shrift to frontiers, and to the balkanization which is everywhere seen, especially by the masses, as a bottleneck.

The stakes are high. But there is no other way to leave behind prehistory and to answer the imperial challenge. The domination of populism, called Arab socialism, has resulted only in dead-ends in all fields of activities. Israel is possible without Zionism, but only a model of a revolutionary society, breaking with both domestic and external obstacles, can obtain such a solution and thereby permit the Arabs to enter history.

Thus we may say that the ideology of Arab nationalism, during the period of history which saw the end of colonialism and the taking-over of the State apparatus and economic decision-making by the petty-bourgeoisie, fulfilled a specific function, but not, however, the one envisaged by Arab progressives. Its main aim, it seems to us, was to legitimize this petty-bourgeoisie in the establishment of a bureaucratic power, by providing the popular mystique that was required. It also provided this class with all the political and ideological excuses needed to block basic doubts about the system, all in the name of Arab unity. As was the case for the ideology of the European bourgeoisies of the 18th century, Arab nationalist ideology conducted a dual struggle: against feudal forces which prevented their access to modernity (capitalism); and against revolutionary demands which opposed a certain type of modernity (socialism). One has to admit that the relationship which existed between the nationalism of a single state (Egypt, Algeria, Iraq, etc.) and Arab nationalism was not one of antagonism (the type of relationship which exists between nationalism and internationalism) but one of ideological complementarity. Arab nationalist ideology has served as a bridge between ancient forms dominated by religious considerations and new forms in which the desire for a centralized state and a purely national economy predominated. This mediating function is explained by the historical situation of the Arab world, its long-time dependence, and the lag which preserved Islam as a defining criterion of the social personality.

As the states grew stronger and as the interests of the Arab bourgeoisies diversified, the transnational ideology fulfilled a new role: to conceal the conflicts between these bourgeoisies, and to justify hegemony under the flag of order and unity.

The transcending of Arab nationalism is not a theoretical but a practical question. What is involved is the eradication of capitalist relationships. It is therefore time to stress anew the priority of social struggles and to reject all socio-political theories which freeze their development. In this perspective, countries which have a strong working-class, and first of all Egypt, will once again play a primary role on the Arab political scene.

A LATIN AMERICAN PERSPECTIVE

Carey Hector

TO raise the issue of inequality in the world system is, to raise the basic question of imperialism. The hierarchical system of accumulation favoured by developed capitalist countries, was instituted through the development of monopolistic capitalism between the end of the 19th century and the beginning of the 20th. Confronted with the evolving dimension of imperialism, one could evaluate the possibilities for development of underdeveloped countries, only on the basis of a dynamic movement against the system's inequalities. This will be the methodological premise of my quick overview of these problems as they relate specifically to Latin America.

First, let me start with the banal observation that some historical traits particular to Latin America should keep us from indiscriminately categorizing it under a catch-all typology of the Third World, simply juxtaposing it with Asia and Africa. Latin American countries acquired their independence by force of arms more than a century and a half ago. There is also the continuous presence of national-democratic movements throughout this period of formal political independence, the relatively high degree of institutional organization, both ideological and political, among several Latin-American bourgeoisies (notably in Chile, Argentina, Brazil and Mexico), and, finally, the differentiated character of Latin American economic development. In short, most Latin American countries would rather fall under the category of "dependent capitalist countries."

As to the international labour movement and Latin American revolutionary movements, let me first emphasize that very little is known of the role played by Latin America within the Third International. It was not until the Fifth Congress of 1924 that a Latin-American Secretariat was created. Even then, only one Latin American member, the Argentinian Codovilla belonged to it along with a Tunisian, a Czech and a Lithunian. In 1928, at the Sixth Congress the Latin-American Secretariat was subdivided in two sections: the Caribbean section under the control of the Communist Party of the U.S.A. and the South-American section located in Buenos Aires and transferred in 1933 to Montevideo. Since that time, the Latin American Communist Parties scrupulously followed the accepted theses on the evolution of colonized and semi-colonized peoples, despite the fact that several Latin-American intellectuals had warned against a mechanical transfer of the International's theses to Latin America. The year 1937 marks the acceptance of the anti-fascist strategy. Latin-American Communist parties also adopted this anti-fascist line, which will come to take priority over an anti-imperialist line. For example, in the Caribbean, there was a policy of alliance with anti-Nazi but pro-imperialist regimes. Similarly, later on, in the 1950's, these movements were totally unable, theoretically and analytically, to understand the specificity of Peronism. With the end of the Cold War, there is a pacifist trend which appears to dominate, appearing in the slogan of peaceful coexistence. In consequence, the Latin-American movement can no longer envisage, even theoretically, the possibility of an autonomous revolution. It was only after the 1960 Moscow conference of Communist parties that a new thesis emerged that was to be followed by Latin American C.P.'s, that of *national democratic front* or the alliance with the national bourgeoisie, the progressive petty bourgeoisie and some segments of the poor peasantry. Between 1960 and 1969, the Cuban revolution occurred and the Tri-Continental conference was held which explains why, nine years later, the new Moscow declaration of the C.P.'s gave special consideration to Latin-America, suggesting the possibility of continuing several forms of struggle, including revolutionary violence. In the mid-1960's, the strategy of popular front reappears, whose tragic fruits were to be seen in Chile. This strategy came about as a consequence of the failures caused by the mechanical transfer of the Cuban model to the whole of Latin America, which then reopened the whole question of alliances.

I should now like to link what precedes with revolutionary movements, the movements aiming at political transformation. I shall not attempt to draw up a balance-sheet of these movements, for no single person could do it. Some general comments are in order however. Faced with the global and unified strategy of the United States, i.e. the anti-subversive strategy that is found at all levels, political, military, cultural and economic, there is a growing awareness in Latin America of the need for a continental strategy to wage the struggle for transformation of its dependent economic and social-political structures. One can remember the recent creation of a junta for revolutionary coordination between the movements of Chile, Argentina, Bolivia and Uruguay. Secondly, there is an increasing sense of the particularity of Latin American movements compared to those in the rest of the world. Here I am only restating what left-wing forces in Latin America have said and what has been repeated by R. Debray in his latest work on Latin-American revolutionary movements. On the one hand, Latin-American revolutionary movements cannot be assimilated to national liberation movements in that the constitution of a nation-state through achieving political independence is not their goal. On the other hand, one cannot reduce Latin-American revolutionary movements to the anti-capitalist struggle of the developed countries, which most socialist or labour parties as well as union leaders wage against State monopolistic capitalism. In Latin America there is a specific combination of class struggle and national struggle. This accounts for the ambiguities of these movements and the trial and error approach they use to establish the right tactical-strategic mix. This also explains the varying programmes of these movements, the combination between so-called democratic tasks, i.e. expansion of political participation of the people, and struggles for social and economic objectives.[1]

Given these general characteristics, the questions raised by Latin American movements center around the following themes. What are the "relevant" class alliances? That is, what combination of classes can lead the anti-imperialist struggle? What class combination could pave the way to the structural transformations which would enable Latin America to withdraw from the world system's inequalities. The second type of question centers around the type of possible struggle. We are far from the usual dichotomous choice: armed struggle vs. peaceful struggle. The last ten to fifteen years

have been extremely useful in stimulating reflection on the historically right combination of long-run and short-run objectives, given
the constraint of each country's specificities (for example, in a country as well known for its labour disputes as Bolivia, the forces of
change cannot adopt the same line of combat as would be applicable, say in Paraguay or in the Central American republics.) Chile's
experience was, once again, illuminating in this respect.

From the Bandung Conference in 1955 to the Non-Aligned
Conference of Algiers in 1973, via the Tri-Continental of 1966, not to
mention the UNCTAD conferences, Latin America has always
played a leading role, sometimes fundamental in clarifying the problems of the Third World facing the world capitalist system. Given its
historical and geographic proximity to the dominant core of the
world system, — given too its lengthy "experience" of that system,
— it seems certain that the example of Latin America will be re-
membered by other countries of the Third World.

NOTE

(1) Saverio Tutino, *L'octobre cubain*, (Paris, Maspéro, 1969-and Régis Debray, *La Critique des
Armes*, I, (Paris, Seuil, 1974), on whom I relied for material on Latin America's role in the
Third International.

WORKING-CLASS MOVEMENTS IN THE ADVANCED AND THIRD WORLD COUNTRIES

Bogdan Denitch

I will begin these notes by pointing out that there is something peculiar and archaic about a book that discusses imperialism, the world market, and the problem of development, but which leaves out the entire question of the working-class parties and their strategies in the metropolitan countries. This is obviously in part a reflection of the current state of the Socialist and Communist movements in the advanced countries, and the tendency for the discussions of the prospect of revolutionary transformation for *both* advanced and underdeveloped societies is to leave them out as potential actors. For several decades intellectuals have been in search of a new set of characters for the revolutionary script. These have ranged from a demobilizing emphasis on the blind forces of economic and social development, to marginal groups such as the lumpenproletariat, the unemployed and the poor, sometimes the students and the revolutionary grouplets, to ethnic minorities, revolutionary feminists and even to the Third World as a potential revolutionizing force for the metropolitan countries.

Obviously this state of affairs is a reflection of a profound pessimism about the prospects of basic structural transformation occurring in the advanced industrial countries through the action of mass working-class-based parties. A side consequence has been that an even greater burden has been historically assigned to our colleagues and friends in the Third World countries whence they are expected not only to build more just and more dynamic societies under appallingly difficult conditions but are also apparently expected to pull our chestnuts out of the fire.

Two background factors are generally cited for a pessimistic prognosis about the prospects of working class parties assuming a political and social offensive. The first, much celebrated in Western social science literature, stresses the structural changes in the character of the work force and celebrates much too prematurely the end of an industrial era based fundamentally on blue collar workers. This particular tendency projects a future in which the overwhelming majority of the employed are going to be white collar professionals or people working in service industries. This tendency then neatly identifies our present with this potential future. Consequently it speaks of an end of ideology, of an end to class conflict, and of the increasingly middle class character of advanced industrial societies. Recently, however, various empirical analyses have put these contentions in serious doubt. To begin with, the absolute number of blue collar manual workers in most advanced industrial countries *has not* declined by more than a negligible percentage. (There are approximately 3% fewer manual blue collar workers in the American work force in 1970 than there were in the 1920's). The number of blue collar manuals remains around 40% of *all* workers male and female. The figure is considerably higher for male only. This figure is fairly constant for all advanced industrial societies and to it should be added the fact that a number of other categories of employees now work under factory-like conditions and are increasingly open to trade union organization. In fact, some of the more militant unions in the advanced industrial countries are found among technicians, municipal employees, teachers, and other groups traditionally not thought of as susceptible to class organizations.

Second, the character of the work force has changed to be sure, but it has changed in a way that is hardly conducive to long-range social stability. As the work in factories continued to become more and more routinized and alienating, the work force in all advanced industrial countries became increasingly more educated, and therefore less likely to accept as legitimate a system of economic and political authority which strips them of the ability to do meaningful and creative work. It is not an accident that it is the younger and the better educated workers who have a greater tendency toward wildcat strikes and towards raising strategic questions which go beyond the classic trade union strategy.

A political factor is often cited. It involves the thesis that the mass working class parties and their institutions are hopelessly encapsulated in the political and social value nexus of their respective societies. A simpler way of putting it is that since the '40's there has been little evidence of working class parties' militancy in western Europe. I would argue that this is in part the effect of the split in the working class parties between the Communists and Social Democrats, and the paralyzing effect of the cold war on the strategy of both those parties. It is clear, however, that this historical split is becoming increasingly politically irrelevant for the working class parties of western Europe. The primacy of domestic politics over the needs of the two major imperialist blocs — the U.S. and the Soviet Union — has revitalized both the Communist and Socialist parties in Europe and created inexorable pressures for unified political and economic action. Thus in Italy and France the Socialist and Communist parties function as political blocs, join hands in local administrations, and have created what is to all practical purposes a reunified single trade union movement which includes the former Catholic trade unions as well. The European Common Market itself exerts a pressure on the Communist and Socialist parties to develop a common supra-national strategy to deal with the common problems of multi-national corporations and Europe-wide strategy of finance capital.

This tendency towards unified action has been accelerated since the late 1960's by a growing polycentrism within the Communist bloc, and by the correct perception which the European Communist leaders have that the Soviet Union has, for practical purposes, abandoned hope in their abilities to become ruling parties, and therefore prefers to deal with the established power structures. One need only remember the behavior of the Soviet ambassador and the attitude of the Soviet press in the last extremely close election in France. The official press of the Communist Part of France openly protested what appeared to be covert Soviet support for the other side.

The trend towards greater independence and toward responsiveness from pressures from below will in all probability increase if for no other reason than that the Communist Parties of Europe are increasingly composed of members who joined in the post-Stalin era and for whom the Soviet Union is neither a socialist paradise nor a center of world strategy but rather a distant, increasingly distant, embarrassment. A part of this is explained of course by the greater level of communication between eastern and western Europe, by the increasing tendency of the Italian and French parties to denounce repression, strike-breaking, anti-Semitism, persecution of intellectuals, and other forms of Soviet behavior which all constitute a problem when they try to project an image of socialism acceptable to their members and voters. In short, the Communists of western Europe have an increased stake in asserting and giving substance to their independence. All this means is that the Communist parties are turning increasingly into left-wing versions of classic social-democratic parties and that there is no real principled obstacle to their continued cooperation with European social democracies. The pan-European aspect of working class strategy thus ends up creating informal alliances where the Italian CP, or more specifically its trade-unions, now maintain excellent relations with the German Social-Democratic party, and where American observers note with dismay that the British Trade Union Congress acts not as a junior partner of the U.S. in the cold war but as an opponent of U.S. policies.

The internationalization of the problem of working class strategy in Europe is only underlined by one specific problem which links their strategy to the economic and social problems of some developing countries. There are today over ten million workers in Europe who are migrants. As a percentage of the work force this varies from country to country, but there is here a phenomenon approaching the scale of that of immigrant labour in the U.S. at the beginning of the century. While a large percentage of these immigrants do, as tradition dictates, the dirty, hard, low-paid work of those societies, an increasing proportion are skilled and integrated into the local trade unions. This means on the one hand that what happens in terms of working class strategies in advanced countries of western Europe has a direct effect on the economies of Greece, Yugoslavia,

Spain, Portugal, Turkey, Tunisia and Algeria, and on the other hand that those "less developed countries" find themselves with an increasingly large and externally-oriented proletarianized mass which has been exposed to the political and economic strategies relevant to advanced industrial politics. What the effect of this is likely to be on labor unrest and the formation of class-oriented politics in the countries from which the migrants come is too soon to predict, but one can speculate on the possibility that as this process continues, politicized Marxist trade union militants will be reimported into their countries of origin *and* that the source of recruitment in an attempt to get a docile and manageable work population may well expand to include more countries from Asia and Africa. Therefore the problem of the relationship of advanced working class parties to the development in the Third World ceases to be only a relatively abstract concern with the world market and imperialism, and becomes a day-to-day question of strategy and tactics. The two are increasingly linked by a world economy and a world market.

These developments all occur in a framework of exhaustion of the standard liberal and Social Democratic paradigms. Inflation, lower rates of economic growth, prospects of unemployment, all spell an end to the previously firmly-held notion that gradual piecemeal reforms were all that was required in the advanced countries of western Europe to maintain and increase the standards of the working class, and to gradually transform those polities into Social-Democratic societies. Everyone today talks about the need for fundamental structural reforms, i.e., for those reforms which go beyond piecemeal economic demands. What is on the agenda is a redistribution of economic and political power and a growing confrontation which challenges the ability of a pluralistic political consensus to defuse class cleavage. The era of relative optimism about the possibility of question concerning the prospects of genuine social revolution in the Third World lay in whether or not there was any prospect for a renewed political offensive by the working class parties in the metropolitan centers, specifically Europe and secondarily the United States. At least for Europe, my answer today is that the prospect now exists, and that we are coming into a period of increasingly sharp class confrontations and cleavages which the present socio-political systems cannot absorb. For that matter, the prospects of renewed working class militancy also exist in eastern Europe and the Soviet Union. There of course it will occur under infinitely more

difficult and challenging conditions but the notion that the bureaucracies can eternally repress a growing increasing skilled and educated working class was always questionable.

To take a step further, one should address oneself to the question of what this means in immediate terms to countries in the middle range of development in the Third World. Growing polycentrism
and the tendency for the U.S. and the Soviet Union to cut back on
their investments in the Third World countries obviously indicate
that a greater effort at utilizing internal resources will be called for
in the near future. Since external aid will lessen this will mean that
the models of development which are meaningfully posed cannot be
those of western Europe or for that matter of the Soviet Union. My
colleague from Algeria, Harbi, has pointed out that Egypt and
Algeria can become neither the Soviet Union nor a China, if for no
other reason than because of the matter of scale. The sheer mas-
siveness of the first two gave them options which do not exist for
most of the Third World countries. I would point out, however, that
they can perhaps conceive of becoming a Yugoslavia — a model
which maintained its independence from the two blocs, accepted aid
from both when available, and which used primarily internal mobilization to develop what is the least repressive and most egalitarian of
the polities calling themselves socialist.

In discussing the prospects of socialist alternatives for Third
World countries, many of us have befuddled the issue by accepting
the claims of a number of the Third World regimes that they are
some variant of socialism. I would argue that these regimes are
anti-colonialist and nationalist, but they are also regimes which are
fundamentally petty-bourgeois, corporatist in the economies, and
repressive vis-à-vis their working classes. In short, that they are regimes which could almost as easily be called fascist as socialist.
What we have to do — if we are to use words in any meaningful
way — is to distinguish sharply between modernizing regimes which
maintain middle class and military elites as ruling strata and those
which seek to base themselves on an activated working class and
peasantry. This is not to deny that the first type of regimes are often
more popular than the ones which they have replaced, but it is no
service to our colleagues in the Third World to accept the claims of
various bureaucratic and military cliques without subjecting them at
least to the same critical scrutiny which we use in analyzing western
Europe, eastern Europe, the Soviet Union and China. I am afraid

that we have tended to fall into the trap of developmentalism. This has meant that we have often assumed that the relative economic and social development of a given country sets absolute and rigid limits as to what political alternatives exist for a given polity. Or, to put it differently, we have depoliticized the whole problem of re-volutionary development and reduced it to economic and social indi-cators without considering the role of parties, leaderships, and strategies. I would instead like to argue for a reintroduction of human will as a factor in the politics of development, and to stress that the range of possible alternatives has never been fully explored. There is a second trap we often fall into and that is the assumption that we live in a universe in which the ruling classes of the advanced countries are all powerful, all knowing, immutable, not subject to class cleavages, economic contradictions and do not make errors. This leads to a fatalistic view of the prospects of revolutionary change which is not justified by any cursory examination even of the last few decades. After all, to take only American imperialism as a case, they can hardly boast of successes in the case of Cuba, in the case of the Indo-Chinese War, and above all in the ability to main-tain a stable world economy which would shore up friendly regimes. Mistakes in strategy are not the exclusive property of the good guys, and we are perhaps entering into a protracted period of social and class conflicts which will bring a major new protagonist to the stage — a revitalized militant working class of the advanced industrial countries.

WORLD INEQUALITY: cultural aspects

CULTURAL LIBERATION AND THE AFRICAN REVOLUTION

Denis Brutus

I would like to assume, though I realize that there are disagreements in matters of definitions, that there is broad agreement on the two elements of the subject: what constitutes liberation and what constitutes culture.

All of Africa is confronted with a similar problem. The degree of dependence may vary, but there is no part of Africa which is not exposed to pressures, to imperialist designs, which is not enmeshed in the imperialist strategy, and therefore all of Africa is confronted with the problem, found also in other parts of the world, of having to deal with the existence of hegemony, of control by super-powers. One would have to distinguish between the situation as it is found in southern Africa and what is loosely called independent Africa. The areas of the continent which are still engaged in an armed struggle against colonial powers, or against a kind of domestic colonialism as in the case of South Africa where the settler and the colonized co-exist, differ in many ways from those parts of Africa which technically enjoy autonomy, but which in fact through economic and political manipulation are still subject to influence from other powers. Although Southern Africa is the area I know best, I will limit myself to just two elements of its situation which seem to me distinctive. In Angola, in Mozambique, in Zimbabwe, in Namibia, in South Africa, in all of those areas, you have people committed to armed struggle. And this is not true of areas of independence. The other element which seems to me significant is that you have in terms of cultural oppression, a systematic attempt through *apartheid*, or the educational systems devised by the ruling minorities, not merely to deny the indigenous people liberation but to subvert their very aspirations. These are programs directed at creating in them an acceptance of dependence, and the notion that this is a permanent and God-willed situation in which they find themselves. That seems to me to distinguish those areas from Nigeria, or Ghana, Kenya, or Uganda.

But there are also certain elements of the struggle for cultural liberation in southern Africa which coincide with elements being found elsewhere in Africa, and I thought it would be useful to enumerate a few of those. One of the most powerful influences in the thinking of Africans, particularly African intellectuals, has been that of Frantz Fanon, and the notion of psychological colonization, which implies the need to decolonize not merely the body and the state, but the mind as well. I would say that there is in Africa now no notion more pervasive, and no notion which seems to me to possess a greater dynamic at this time. There is one other which approximates it, the concept of pan-Africanism, which enjoyed a great vitality at a given period in Africa, and which may well now be due for revival. Fanon would count as one of the most important influences operating on the African mind, on the African intellectual, in setting a direction to (and the recognition of the need for this direction) the decolonization of the mind.

At a gathering similar to this, a colloquium in Brazzaville, in a gathering of African intellectuals, this was taken for granted. It was assumed that this was understood by everyone. And instead a new stage was undertaken, a re-examination of the choices being offered to Africa between a Western capitalist system, ideology, set of values, and a Marxist communist system on the other hand. And after much discussion, much analysis, the consensus was, and I am sure this is familiar to many of you, that for Africa there did not exist this either/or choice, or that it need not accept this either/or choice, that it would be possible instead to find a third, an African way, an African solution. There had been hints of this, of course, in Kwame Nkrumah, the notion of an African personality, of African socialism. There had been an elaboration of these ideas through Julius Nyerere, the concept of *Ujamaa*, of what is now being reformulated I think as Tanzanian rather than African socialism (so that it does not seem a panacea for all of the continent, so that each area might develop its own characteristic economic and social system, derived from the cultural roots and the history of the people.)

The question of pan-Africanism advocated by many, and specifically by Nkrumah, the notion of a Union of African States which gave rise to the Organization of African Unity is being re-examined very much at the present time, and I believe will be the focus, the central issue in the Congress next month in Dar es Salaam, the VIth Pan African Congress. And already in the preliminary discussion and the papers which have circulated, a very interesting point is emerging, the idea that the Organization of African Unity is a contradiction of the concept of pan-Africanism. I think that this is so important that perhaps one ought to spend a little time in showing how this sense of contradiction is arrived at. Among the elements in the argument is the fact that the O.A.U. simply stabilizes and consolidates a state of affairs which is a false reflection of African societies, that nation-states, as at present constituted, exist as a result of artificial and arbitrary boundaries, some of them deriving from the partition of Africa, some of them from subsequent developments. But in this consolidation of states and the formalization thereof in the O.A.U., we are in fact agreeing to attempt to develop from a series of false premises, that if the initial premise was wrong, development derived therefrom must be wrong as well, and inimical to the future development of the continent.

It is I suppose a truism that the people who live in Zaire, and the people who live on the banks of the Congo River, are one people, though there may be some confusion now that the river is called both the Congo and the Zaire. But certainly the barriers which were drawn by colonial powers, whether they were French, English, or German, or Portuguese, or Belgian, are in fact a false reflection of the real situation. It has another important component. The argument is that the idea of pan-Africanism implies a rejection of the colonial relationships which exist. And the leaders of African states are seen as simply an elite to whom power was transferred by the colonial powers as an extension and a continuance of their influence in these countries. I'm reluctant to make a kind of detailed diagnosis of the ills that beset Nigeria, and Ghana, Uganda, Kenya and the others. I trust I can leave that to you. But I ought to say, just to offset that, that many Africans see the developments in Tanzania and Guinea as a counterpoise, as a motion in the opposite and correct direction, that ultimately the cultural liberation of each African nation-state will be based on the kind of premises of equality and an economic and social system derived from the history and culture of the people, a natural outgrowth of that. And, in passing, I should say that, in this ambition, many Africans believe that there is a great deal to be learned from China, and that the example and influence of China must be seen as a growing force for the future.

Where do the cultural practitioners fit into this? What is their specific contribution? I am thinking of creative artists, writers, film makers. They seem to me to fall into several categories, and I might isolate three of these.

The notion of "cultural diplomacy" has a special reference in Africa. We understand the role of imperialism, of cultural imperialism, and in the deformation of minds, in the process of pre-empting, of co-opting people into the system and making them collaborators in the system. But particularly in independent Africa the term "cultural diplomacy" has a different signification and this is the notion that the artist, the cultural producer, should become the apologist of the system, the unofficial roving ambassador, whose function is to project a good image and whose role is to defend the system. This has not worked out because most of the intellectuals have ended as the opponents of the status quo. The outstanding example, I should think, is Wole Soyinka of Nigeria. I would mention specifically his book, *The Man Died*, with its devastating attack on Gowon and the present regime.

But on the other hand, and this is the obverse, one has an Achebe writing in defense of the Biafran cause. The failure here seems to me to be an inability to identify the root causes of the conflict. To explain the Nigerian conflict in terms of tribal rivalries and antagonisms is one level of superficiality, but to say as Soyinka says that it was more than that, it was a collapse of humanity, of human beings behaving in some atavistic fashion, seems to me merely another level of superficiality. Any failure to take into account the rivalries, the economic rivalries of the multinational corporations, of the oil interests, of Western powers causes one to end up with a superficial interpretation. Fortunately there are writers, both critics and creative writers, who have penetrated beyond that and who see the African predicament, or tragedy if you will, in terms of this kind of manipulation of political and economic power for strategic reasons, whatever these reasons might be. I refer to other creative artists, people like James Nguge from Kenya, Peter

Nazareth from Uganda, whose basis for judgment is sometimes overtly Marxist, sometimes a vague kind of socialist judgment, but who at least can discover the underlying forces operating against African liberation, cultural liberation or indeed the larger whole of which cultural liberation is only a segment, the liberation of a people in every area of their existence.

The writers of South Africa among whom I'm included — a La Guma, an Mphalele, an Nkosi — cannot return to their countries, but in a sense the position is no less difficult for a Soyinka in Nigeria or an Achebe or indeed a Kofi Awooner from Ghana. For all of us, the moment we become the gadflies in the society, the moment we become the critics and the commentators on what is projected as an ideal situation, at that moment we must expect to find ourselves in conflict with the situation.

I want to return to the liberation movement. I might have talked about Senghor and negritude as one of the minor little bypaths in the process of cultural evolution, cultural liberation, except that for most Africans today it is either passé or in fact pernicious, something which is harmful to cultural liberation. My last point rather is to say that the significance of the southern African liberation movement is that is goes beyond resistance. It is not resistance to oppression; it is not even liberation merely in the sense of freedom to govern yourself. It has penetrated beyond that to an understanding that what we are engaged in is a struggle against imperialism. It is not a local, nor even a national struggle. We see ourselves as an element in the global struggle against imperialism. This seems to me the truly revolutionary element in our struggle for cultural liberation.

CULTURAL ALIENATION IN FRANCE AND CHINA

Paul-Marie de la Gorce

THE preoccupation in Europe with the cultural dimension of national struggles, and with the confrontation between the dominated and the dominators, between the desire for national liberation and the desire for emancipation, is a very old one. A large part of European history, particularly in the 19th century, is marked by this concern. In particular, central Europe and the Balkans lived through a long period, not too distant, characterized by the struggle for self-determination of the peoples living under Turkish, Austrian, Austro-German, or Russian domination. In the course of their struggles for national liberation, they have spontaneously expressed, sometimes from the start, their will to exist quite specifically as a cultural entity. The right to their language was a fundamental claim. No one can deny that language is the more elementary expression of culture. The right to use one's national language, to write, to teach, to publish was the very first demand addressed to the Austrian and Turkish masters.

We are therefore quite familiar with this fundamental aspect of national liberation movements, the struggle for cultural autonomy. It is a major element of the more general problem of cultural liberation and human liberation. The history of the colonial era provides us with another example, both very illuminating and quite ambiguous. Very illuminating, because one of the forms of resistance to colonization has been the assertion of one's cultural originality, often the attempt to rediscover cultural history, cultural traditions, the socio-cultural origins of the civilization which the colonial system tended to repress or even deny its existence. But this is not the only cultural aspect of the search for liberation of colonized people. Access to the culture of the colonizing country for some elements of the people under tutelage has constituted in some cases an instrument of liberation: this is the dialectical process, well-known to historians of these epochs and problems, whereby the oppressor himself provides the means for his own destruction.

One should examine these two examples at the same time — the European and the colonial — in order to make it very clear that one cannot dissociate the problem of cultural liberation from that of overall liberation, and specifically from that of political liberation. One should not forget either that we may find in the cultural history of the peoples traits which result from the interrelations of dominators and dominated, between colonizers and colonized, between oppressors and oppressed. The problem is complex and marked by reciprocal reactions and interactions. To evoke the contemporary issues of cultural liberation I shall use only two examples, very different ones, the examples of China and France. I do this in part because I know them well, but also because, being so different, they make us realize that the problem of cultural liberation varies with the individual cases, and that it is hard to make global generalizations. Nonetheless, beyond the specificities, there is the "heart" of the problem, which is perhaps the same everywhere.

Everybody has been struck by the fact that one of the greatest political and historical surges of the Chinese revolution has been named a "cultural revolution," or more precisely, the "Great Proletarian Cultural Revolution." We are astonished to see that for the first time a revolution has chosen to call itself a "cultural revolution." It is all the more surprising since what was involved was not prima facie a cultural manifestation linked to specific institutions but rather included economic, political and social elements of prime importance, a question to which we shall return. Therein lies a matter of fundamental importance. The Chinese themselves analyze it with great rigour and place great emphasis on clarifying the question. We must remember that, for them, initiating or developing a phase of the revolution by calling into question the superstructure of the Chinese political and social cultural system clearly underlines the dialectical importance these super-structures have in the overall development of Chinese society. In tackling the super-structures, they are in fact consciously aiming at the global development of Chinese revolutionary society. Indeed, in their view, it is through the super-structures that one can best see the risk of distortion or bad orientation in a revolution. We have there an extraordinarily perceptive acknowledgement of the close links between the most important, most significant, most essential cultural manifestations and the heart of "revolutionary" development. Culture, most particularly through education and teaching, which are its most influential manifestations both in social and economic terms, was seen as a factor of socio-economic stabilization and, in the final analysis, of social stratification. Through certain types of educational systems, the ruling groups might lay roots for their power, and assure their continued presence at the helm of the state, and even of society.

A certain type of teaching and educational system, would give the ruling groups the opportunity to co-opt each other, thanks to the fact that it would become easier for their friends, children and associates to adapt spontaneously to the system. This education, this culture did indeed bear the mark of a specific historic, social and economic situation which had fostered the emergence of such leaders. Their continued presence could only reinforce the differences between social groups and, finally, create some sort of social stratification. In effect, the present Chinese ideology insists on the very strong risks of the re-emergence of such social stratification. It links the phenomena described above to the more or less strong hierarchy of salaries within the firms, to the tendency of giving precedence to certain sectors of the economy over others, to the existence of differences in standards of life and, even more, in life-patterns between the city and the country, between manual workers and intellectual workers. In other words, to use their own language (not necessarily ours), through this development of social stratification, a process permitted by a certain socio-cultural system, and which is at issue. In this case, the Chinese do not hesitate to talk of "the restoration of capitalism".

The solution they adopted to resist what they consider a mortal peril for their revolution is well-known. I will only mention some of its most important features. First, there is what I would call, without seeking to be derogatory, its totalitarian nature, extraordinarily striking and visible, for example, in the choice of texts for reading materials, the phrases that are repeated in foreign languages, the very particular way of teaching history, etc. I do not need to press the point, though we should keep it in mind, for it would be impossible to understand the true meaning of the system if we didn't recognize this fundamental aspect of the cultural system presently prevailing in China. The second feature is the content of curricula. We don't have the time to go into a detailed difference between the Chinese and Western systems. The nearly complete eradication of the study of philosophy and of traditional literature, the practical and political side of instruction, are readily apparent, along with the desire to integrate Western technology, to consistently link the experimental and theoretical, the practical and the conceptual. At the same time, the length of higher education has been reduced. The third feature is the highly selective operation of the system with difficult, rigorous firm decisions taken jointly by university and political authorities. The fourth, and by far the most important feature is obviously the link between study and work. To the Chinese it is fundamental. It is essential according to them for the destruction (let us not hesitate to use the word) of the old cultural system. This explains the interruption of studies for periods of from six to twelve months, for work either in factories or in the countryside. This system applies not only to students but to many professors as well who spend many months of their life doing simple kinds of work. We know the ideological background to these measures. We also know that it is essential in the Chinese view, and that it has a more general importance, since it tries, by the interpenetration of social categories at all levels of cultural and educational development, to insure the necessary amalgam of people of various occupations, and to abolish the barriers that rapidly emerge between highly educated people and the balance of the population. In sum, it is through this continuous process of questioning the cultural and educational system, through this radical condemnation, sometimes violent, of traditional cultural and educational frameworks, that a true and fundamental step forward of revolutionary development may materialize. The Chinese themselves maintain that is but one stage; other stages will follow. In this respect the campaign against Confucianism is characteristic. It attacks a certain mode of traditional education, a certain way of relating life and nature.

Finally, the struggle against the distortions between the industrial and the rural world, between manual and intellectual work, is essential in terms of the Chinese conception of cultural emancipation, and of human liberation, which they call "revolution." It is only fair in this instance to remind ourselves of the passages in Marx when he announced that at the end of the prehistory in which we are presently living, and in contrast to the real history which he believes men will know when there are no more class struggles, when the bourgeoisie will have disappeared, manual and intellectual work will at last be one.

It may sound paradoxical to follow up these very short comments with a brief analysis of the French case. I shall not try to lead you in the wild domain of French controversies on national educational policy. Even Frenchmen are reserved on this point. I just want to mention the cultural problem in France from the standpoint of the emancipation and human freedom we are discussing. The first characteristic is what I call the high degree of nationalization of culture in France. Undoubtedly, this is a country, a society where, in one way or another, the culture produced by the few, and perhaps for the few, has been widely adopted by all social strata. We cannot say that Molière or Victor Hugo belong to a particular stratum of Frenchmen, even if we know they emerged in a specific historical context. What I call nationalization of culture in France is an essential phenomenon in terms of the issue of cultural liberation in a country like France. This fact has been made even more true by the massive spread of culture via the mass media. We make no judgment here about the value of the cultural content or its meaning. Let us stick to the same simple facts. One play by Racine played one evening on television has as many persons watching as in 300 years since it was written. That is not a minor fact. The fact that the media are today such a powerful transmitter of "acculturation" for nearly everyone cannot be discounted lightly. Again, I want to avoid discussing the content, the evolution of the culture, or the impact of the media on this culture. The phenomenon we have noted is manifestly extremely important. Were we to ignore it, we could not understand the French cultural system as a whole.

Given this phenomenon, a host of new problems arise, among which I shall discuss two. One is the importance rightly attached in a society like France to the age at which cultural and educational learning begins. This explains the immense growth of educational programs for children 3 to 6 years old, and the development of kindergarten education which France, more than any other industrial country, has experienced in the last few years. The second problem is the following: whatever the efforts made to facilitate access to high-school education for an increasing percentage (85%) of children from the Paris area, whatever the efforts of all kinds made to increase the already impressively large student population, it has been gradually discovered that it is impossible to reduce the differences in aptitudes, opportunities, development and, more generally, access to culture of citizens, and that it was therefore of paramount importance that, during the course of life, one should be able continuously to reopen, the early decisions of the educational system. Therein lies the fundamental importance given in recent years in France to continuing education.

I can only conclude with a pair of seemingly contradictory statements. First, there are considerable differences between one cultural situation and another, and it is therefore impossible to conceive of a single model for cultural liberation. The specific characteristics of cultural alienation are so obvious and so strong that one cannot really imagine such a single model. However, on the other hand, there is the simple recognition that, in the last analysis, there always exists a cultural dimension to the problem of man's liberation. It is up to our times or our generation to grasp its true importance.

CULTURAL NATIONALISM VS. CULTURAL REVOLUTION: ARGENTINA, QUÉBEC AND CHINA

Jorge Niosi

AS a sociologist concerned with the analysis of dependent countries such as Canada and Argentina, without, however, having specialized in cultural aspects of dependence, I think it is important to note the intensity with which the themes of cultural sovereignty, of cultural autonomy, or even of "cultural revolution" are developed in these countries, both at the level of political ideology and the ideology propagated by the "social sciences." In Québec, as in Argentina (and in many other countries in the periphery), there is much talk about cultural sovereignty, cultural autonomy and even cultural revolution. I shall try first to explain the intensity of the resurgence of these themes in contemporary political and scientific ideology. I should also like to take exception to what Mr. de la Gorce said about the universal validity of the Chinese model in cultural terms.

These themes of cultural autonomy, national culture or cultural sovereignty which, in Argentina, are expounded by the nationalist party in power, the Peronist party, is a party which represents a class alliance between national capitalists and the organized working class. This theme has been systematically developed in Argentina with the re-emergence of the Peronist movement, both in terms of party propaganda and through the writings of social scientists who argue in favour of building a national culture through a cultural revolution from the top. In Canada, particularly in Québec, these same themes are current. Of course, the situation in Argentina and Québec is quite different. In Canada, the social agent which propounds this ideology is the party of an oppressed national minority, but one that speaks nonetheless to the same social classes: national entrepreneurs and the organized working class. The differences, of course, are very important. In the Argentine case there is a nationalist party, lead by nationalist petty bourgeois and the middle strata bourgeois, who are in power in a country which, de jure at least, is independent. In Canada, this national phenomenon, these themes of cultural autonomy, appear in a country with two nations, where the minority oppressed nation does not hold power and where its party is in opposition. In both cases however there is one more common feature: both national movements are lead by peripheral national bourgeoisies, thus by weak groups that are incapable of imposing their hegemony on the whole society. In both cases, the themes of cultural autonomy, cultural sovereignty, appear dissociated from economic autarky or from full political autonomy. In Québec the nationalist party talks about political autonomy within an economic union with Canada; in Argentina the nationalist party in power has abandoned altogether the idea of political or economic autarky. The reason for couching the national phenomenon exclusively in cultural terms is found precisely in the extreme weakness of these national bourgeoisies in countries which cannot follow an autonomous capitalist path. *Lacking the power to lead a bourgeois revolution on the political and economic fronts, the petite bourgeoisie makes or rather attempts to make a cultural revolution.* In both cases, there are some ideological components borrowed from the Chinese cultural revolution as though the situations were comparable. This is a case of an ideological attempt by these populist movements to capitalize on the prestige of the Chinese revolution in order to bridge the gap with more radical elements of the movement. This is clearly the case with Peronism.

Let us now see the differences between the above two cases and the Chinese revolution by trying out the reverse of Mr. de la Gorce's hypothesis. I suggest that, in the Chinese cultural revolution, there are many elements of universal value which apply to all Third World countries — the countries at the periphery of the world capitalist system.

What are the essential differences? First, a historical difference. The Chinese cultural revolution did not occur between 1966 and 1969. On the contrary the whole movement goes back to the beginning of the Chinese revolution, with the first struggles against Japan. For instance, in the 1930's the phrase, cultural revolution, appears in connection with the first campaigns in favour of land redistribution. In the early 1940's, there is a campaign of cultural rectification and rectification among the cadres. In 1956, there is the movement in favour of thought reform among intellectuals and 1951 and 1952 saw the campaign of the "three anti's" — i.e., anti-corruption, anti-waste and anti-bureaucracy. In 1957, there is the reform and rectification campaign against the state and party bureaucracies. The Chinese cultural revolution movement is not an autonomous movement, nor is it a movement separated from the more global movement of the military, political and economic revolutions. On the contrary, it is an integral part of these more global movements. It essentially aims at changing the nature of production relationships within Chinese society, at the institution of a socialist mode of production. It seeks also, and this is the heart of the difference with the other situations, to change the social situation of intellectuals through a reduction in the social division of labour (a division which Mr. de la Gorce emphasized) the division between manual and intellectual work. This trend towards a cultural renovation in China also aims at eliminating the market ideology, the liberal ideology according to which each individual behaving rationally and independently would maximize his satisfaction, his utilities as well as those of the whole of society. Another difference: Chinese culture and the cultural revolution are multinational. The Chinese cultural revolution is applicable to all nationalities forming the Chinese people. It aims in fact at suppressing differences and at the cultural unification of the country. The Chinese model of cultural revolution is thus an integral part of a larger movement of political and economic revolution. The model works for socialism; it is thus multi-national.

This point is rather important in terms of being the universal element in liberation of the peripheral countries. Indeed one cannot think now of a political or economic revolution which would not be multinational, which would not encompass several dependent countries. Confronted with the hegemony within the world capitalist system of two super-powers, the U.S. and the USSR, underdeveloped countries cannot stay divided or try to liberate themselves separately. They cannot imagine either that some cultural liberation could come about without an accompanying economic and political revolution. From that perspective, taking into account all its characteristics (total rupture with the capitalist mode of production, its multinational nature, radical transformation of the social situation of intellectuals), the Chinese revolution offers a model to all dependent countries, despite what Mr. de la Gorce thinks. It appears less plausible every day that one oppressed and dependent nation could alone today destroy the hegemony of the U.S. or the USSR except through a transnational movement, that would seek *simultaneously* cultural, economic and political liberation.

THE PARTICULAR AND UNIVERSAL IN THE CHINESE CULTURAL REVOLUTION

Mohamed-Salah Sfia

IN all the other cultural experiences — Arab nationalism, Arab socialism, pan-Africanism, negritude, African socialism, Latin-Americanism (if we may use this term), etc. — the leitmotiv is a demand for identity, self-assertion, the expression of a desire to recover something called cultural personality, national culture, special genius, etc. The inherent logic underlying such an attitude is one of opposition to the other, to the stranger, etc. By this I do not imply, as many have too often done, that it is chauvinism or xenophobia which is behind these cultural-national movements. I am merely saying that these trends reflect in some way the great need to define oneself as different from others, as having an original identity, irreducible to that of another. The moving force behind this type of ideology is thus typically a claim of *particularism*. It entails proclaiming one's own cultural *particularity* to others. A movement such as Arab nationalism, for example, developed a line of argument which was something like this: We are people, or a group of peoples, with our own history, our own culture, etc. We thus assert our particularities as Arabs as opposed to Europeans, Chinese, Indians, Africans.

Moreover, and this is most important, this assertion of a given cultural specificity which, as we mentioned, is a *particularist* assertion, is used ideologically as a *universal* response to *universal* questions. When one says to the Arab nationalist, to the African socialist, "There are *universal* problems of the organization of society, of the development of its productive forces. To these *universal* problems a *universal* response has been given, for example Marxism. The response may be good or bad, but it can only be accepted or rejected on the basis of its *universality* as a possible effective response to certain problems of social organization," one gets the following response: "I reject this solution, as it is foreign to me. It is not Arab, African, etc. It is not adapted to my particular situation. I am neither a Marxist nor a capitalist, I am an Arab, an African, etc."

Not only is the approach of Chinese Cultural Revolution different from the above described one, but it is in fact diametrically opposed. For it is quite clear that the struggle carried on by some social groups in China and later called the Cultural Revolution or the Great Proletarian Cultural Revolution makes no reference whatsoever to these claims of identity or of specificity. The main concern of the makers of the Chinese Cultural Revolution was not to say to the rest of the world "We are Chinese, we are different, we have our own specificity." They were not overwhelmed by the thought of foreign influences which could, *as such*, as foreign, threaten them as Chinese. The logic of Chinese revolutionaries has been totally different. It is a profoundly *universalist* logic, a class logic. What they say is: "The problem is to revolutionize the structure of society in a direction favourable to the interests of certain classes, the popular classes. The problem is the struggle to substitute new social relations for previous ones. The struggle must be carried on at several levels, among which is the cultural or the ideological one. The Cultural Revolution is precisely the concrete manifestation of this struggle at the ideological level." The Chinese who are identified with the Cultural Revolution do not say, "Given the problem of Chinese society's destiny, this is a *Chinese* solution which we wish to promote." Quite to the contrary, they say: "Given the problem of the future of Chinese society, *which is not unique but only one case among others* (despite certain specific traits), this is the *socialist, revolutionary, proletarian* solution which we wish to promote." One may clearly see that to a universal question is given the most *universal* possible response.

In other words, cultural movements such as Arab nationalism, African socialism, are movements which, even if they are sometimes progressive (leading an anti-imperialist struggle at certain moments, for example), appear fundamentally motivated by non-revolutionary objectives: the *recovery* and *conservation* of a culture, a personality, a specificity. These are the underlying themes and basically they express a fear of change, self-overprotection, in short conservatism, rather than a forward look. Nowadays there is probably nothing as daring, as dynamic, as committed to changing social and mental structures, in short, as *revolutionary* and *radical* in its will to change, as the movement of the Chinese Cultural Revolution.

It thus appears evident that one should distinguish carefully these two types of experiences, the Chinese Revolution and the others mentioned above. Even if they are grouped together in a category called "cultural movements," they are totally different one from the other. The difference may be summarized as follows: the Chinese are only interested in the struggle of social classes, including at the world level, while the others are still concerned with the struggle between nations and cultures.

NOTES ON THE CONTRIBUTORS

Ervand Abrahamian, Dept. of History, City University of New York. Author of many articles on Iran in *Past and Present*, *Middle Eastern Studies*, and the *International Journal of Middle East Studies*.

Dennis Brutus, South African poet and activist, Dept. of English, Northwestern University.

Paul Marie de la Gorce, French author, and formerly an aide to the Prime Minister.

Bogdan Denitch, Dept. of Sociology, Queens College (CUNY) and Research Associate, Bureau of Applied Social Research.

Mohamed Dowidar, Dept. of Political Economy, Law School, University of Alexandria (Egypt). Author, *L'économie politique, une science sociale*. Former professor, University of Algiers.

Mohamed Harbi, University of Paris (Vincennes). Former editor, Révolution africaine, Algiers.

Cary Hector, Dept. of Political Science, University of Québec in Montreal. Born in Haiti.

Albert-Paul Lentin, University of Paris (Vincennes). Author, *La lutte tricontinentale*.

Jorge Niosi, Dept. of Sociology, University of Québec in Montreal. Born in Argentina.

Jean Piel, National Center of Scientific Research, Paris. Many writings on Peru.

Mohamed-Salah Sfia, Dept. of Sociology, University of Montreal. Born in Tunisia.

Immanuel Wallerstein, Dept. of Sociology, McGill University. Author, *The Modern World-System*.

Mel Watkins, Dept. of Political Economy, University of Toronto.

Richard D. Wolff, Dept. of Economics, University of Massachusetts, Amherst. Author, *The Economics of Colonialism: Britain and Kenya, 1870-1930*.

THE POLITICAL ECONOMY OF THE STATE
Canada/Québec/USA

edited by
Dimitrios
Roussopoulos

The book contains a series of major essays examining the State. These include *"The Fiscal Crisis of the State in Canada"* by Rick Deaton, *"The Growth of the State in Québec"* by B. Roy Lemoine, *"Authority and the State"* by Graeme Nicholson, *"Revolution in the Metropolis"* by Margaret and John Rowntree, and *"The State as socializer"* by Lorne Huston.

The Political Economy of the State begins an important new approach to the study of government and society which political science has ignored for a very long time.

"This book should be mandatory reading... it is a valuable contribution to literature on the modern state... *The Political Economy of the State* does a workmanlike and effective job in its demolition of the myth of the state as a benevolent force in society..."
— Bob Bettson, *The Varsity*

200 pages with charts / Hardcover $10.95 / Paperback $2.95
 ISBN: 0-919618-02 / ISBN: 0-919618-01-4

Chosen for *Canadian Basic Books*

BLACK ROSE BOOKS No. D 8

QUEBEC LABOUR

Preface by
Marcel Pépin,
president
of the CNTU

What is the Confederation of National Trade Unions (CNTU) in Québec? How did it develop from its Catholic origins into a mass militant trade union movement representing 250,000 workers? How does the CNTU differ from the AFL-CIO affiliated Québec Federation of Labour? How did the CNTU move beyond collective bargaining to become a unique trade movement in North America? What is the CNTU's SECOND FRONT and what has been its effect in radicalizing both the organised labour force in Québec and the working population in general?

Why has the CNTU now adopted a uniquely anti-imperialist, socialist, and workers' control policy? What is the relationship of the CNTU to the national liberation movement in Québec? How does the CNTU analyse the 'Quiet Revolution'?

These and other questions are dealt with in this book, the content of which include:

A long historical introduction, the official translation of the document of the SECOND FRONT, and the exclusive official translation of the historic, *"Ne comptons que sur nos propres moyens"*.

2nd Revised Edition
224 pages / Hardcover $10.95 / Paperback $3.95
ISBN: 0-919618-14-6 / ISBN: 0-919618-15-4

Chosen for *Canadian Basic Books*

BLACK ROSE BOOKS No. C 6
Library of Congress Catalog Card Number: 73-76058

SPHERES OF INFLUENCE IN THE THIRD WORLD

This second volume of papers submitted to the Bertrand Russell Centenary Symposium in Linz, Austria, includes contributions by Bipan Chandra, Malcolm Caldwell, Edward W. Said and James F. Petras, with H. Michael Erisman and Charles Mills, on spheres of influence policies of great powers in much of the third world. There is also an important paper by Vladimir Dedijer tracing the development of the concept of spheres of influence.

023 / 123 pages / SBN 85124 060 7
Paperback $4.95

ESSAYS ON SOCIALIST HUMANISM,
in honour of the Centenary of Bertrand Russell
EDITED BY KEN COATES

Contributors include Jean Paul Sartre, Vladimir Dedijer, Noam Chomsky, Lelio Basso, Mihailo Markovic and many others.

"How important... that the publishers should have brought out a volume to honour the Centenary of Bertrand Russell's birth and to explore the relationship between Russell's liberalism, libertarianism and pacifism and recent trends in the socialist movement. Great riches of social and political philosophy are to be found here, and that is not surprising... A very rewarding volume... and a whole range of writers combine a well-knit series of essays."
— *Times Literary Supplement*

021 / 220 pages / SBN 85124 047x
Hardcover $10.00

SPHERES OF INFLUENCE IN THE AGE OF IMPERIALISM

A first volume of papers submitted to the Bertrand Russell Centenary Symposium in Linz, Austria, Contributors include Noam Chomsky, Ernest Mandel, Lelio Basso, Mihailo Markovic, Michael Barrat Brown and Marily B. Young, who presented text on the theory of imperialism, contradictions and assessment of two phases of U.S. imperialism.

022 / 144 pages / SBN 85124 059 3
Paperback $4.95

A TRADE UNION STRATEGY
EDITED BY KEN COATES

This book is a translation of the Workers' Control programme adopted by the Belgian trade union movement (FGTB) at their 1971 congress. It is the only book in English that highlights the major advances being made by a trade union centre that has often blazed a path for the whole of European trade unionism. Ken Coates outlines the Belgian situation, M.B. Brown deals with the public accountability of companies, and Louis de Brouckere deals with how workers' control can be set up.

010 / 149 pages   **SBN 85124 023 2**
                                   Hardcover $4.95

ESSAYS ON IMPERIALISM
BY MICHAEL BARRAT BROWN

There are four major essays, "A Critique of Marxist Theories of Imperialism", "The Stages of Imperialism", "Imperialism and Working Class Interests in the Developed Countries", and "The E.E.C. and Neo-Colonialism in Africa". The essays are a major intervention into the debate between Sweezy, Jalee, Magdoff and Mandel, among others, as to whether capitalist countries will remain united in their joint efforts to exploit the Third World, or split into warring competitive factions. Barrat Brown argues that both views have limitations.

011 / 163 pages   **SBN 85124 024 0**
                                   Hardcover $9.95

READINGS IN AMERICAN IMPERIALISM
EDITED BY K.T. FANN & DONALD C. HODGES

America's increasing involvement in the affairs of other countries has led many to question her motivations and purposes in defending interests abroad. This selection of essays examines the theory of imperialism inherent in capitalism, and discusses American economic and political involvement in South America, and its effects on Third World countries. Also discussed is the reaction to and effects of U.S. imperialism in the home country, and reactions of Third World spokesmen. Articles by Theodore Dos Santos, Conor Cruise O'Brien, Paul Baran, Harry Magdoff, Paul Sweezy, Fidel Castro, Lin Pao, and Che Guevara, among others, provide a comprehensive view of what many consider a basic policy inherent in this kind of social and economic structure which is antithetical to world-wide cooperation and human development.

04 / 384 pages / paperback $5.95 / $9.95 hardcover
Extending Horizons Series

ESSAYS ON MARX'S THEORY OF VALUE
by Isaak Illich Rubin

According to the prevailing theories of economists, economics has replaced political economy, and economics deals with scarcity, prices, and resource allocation. In the definition of Paul Samuelson, "economics — or political economy, as it used to be called... is the study of how men and society *choose,* with or without the use of money, to employ *scarce* productive resources, which could have alternative uses, to produce various commodities over time and distribute them for consumption, now and in the future, among various people and groups in society."

If economics is indeed merely a new name for political economy, and if the subject matter which was once covered under the heading of political economy is now covered by economics, then economics has replaced political economy. However, if the subject matter of political economy is not the same as that of economics, then the "replacement" of political economy is actually an omission of a field of knowledge. If economics answers different questions from those raised by political economy, and if the omitted questions refer to the form and the quality of human life within the dominant social-economic system, then this omission can be called a "great evasion".

Economic theorist and historian I. I. Rubin suggested a definition of political economy which has nothing in common with the definition of economics quoted above. According to Rubin, "Political economy deals with human working activity, not from the standpoint of its technical methods and instruments of labor, but from the standpoint of its social form. It deals with *production relations* which are established among people in the process of production." In terms of this definition, political economy is not the study of prices or of scarce resources; it is a study of social relations, a study of culture.

Rubin's book was first published in the Soviet Union, and was never re-issued after 1928. This is the first and only English edition. The translators are Milos Samardzija and Fredy Perlman.

275 pages / Hardcover $10.95 / Paperback $3.95
ISBN: 0-919618-11-1 / ISBN: 0-919618-18-9

BLACK ROSE BOOKS No. D 13

THE UNKNOWN REVOLUTION 1917-1921

by Voline

Introduction by Rudolph Rocker

This famous history of the revolution in Russia and its aftermath has been long out of print. The present edition combined the previous two-volume English-language edition plus omitted material from later editions. It is a complete translation of La revolution inconnue, first published in French in 1947, and re-published in Paris in 1969 by Editions Pierre Belfond.

Voline was both a social historian and educator during this period as well as an active revolutionary. He writes and researches this history from a point of view which covers the achievements of ordinary people and not of this political party or other. It is a libertarian analysis written by a famous anarchist, and a kind of history not read in our schools.

717 pages, illustrated | Hardcover $16.95 | Paperback $4.95
ISBN: 0-919618-26-X/ISBN: 0-919618-25-1

BLACK ROSE BOOKS No. E 29